Write It Real

This book is part of the Peter Lang Education list.
Every volume is peer reviewed and meets
the highest quality standards for content and production.

PETER LANG
New York • Bern • Berlin
Brussels • Vienna • Oxford • Warsaw

Dan Valenti

Write It Real

A Practical Guide for the Prose Writer

PETER LANG
New York • Bern • Berlin
Brussels • Vienna • Oxford • Warsaw

Library of Congress Cataloging-in-Publication Control Number: 2022008466

Bibliographic information published by **Die Deutsche Nationalbibliothek**.
Die Deutsche Nationalbibliothek lists this publication in the "Deutsche
Nationalbibliografie"; detailed bibliographic data are available
on the Internet at http://dnb.d-nb.de/.

ISBN 978-1-4331-9282-1 (paperback)
ISBN 978-1-4331-9279-1 (ebook pdf)
ISBN 978-1-4331-9280-7 (epub)
DOI 10.3726/b19646

2022 Peter Lang Publishing, Inc., New York
80 Broad Street, 5th floor, New York, NY 10004
www.peterlang.com

For my loving and loved wife, Lisa Marie Valenti.
To Lucy and Smokey, our saints.
In memoriam, Gary Van Dusen, dear friend and respected colleague.

"One day, I will find the right words, and they will be simple"—Jack Kerouac, from *The Dharma Bums*

Table of Contents

Foreword

There's a scene in a 1966 movie starring Paul Newman and Richard Boone. The movie, *Hombre*, pits Newman in the title role, John Russell, with Boone as Grimes, the proverbial "bad guy." In the scene, Russell voluntarily walks into a deadly trap to rescue and free a captive woman. Grimes and his henchmen have him in their sights.

Grimes, responding to Russell's combination of courage and recklessness, addresses him: "They said you've got a lot of hard bark on you, walking down here like this. ... Now what do you suppose hell is going to look like?"

Newman: "We all die. Just a question of when."

Following the exchange, gunfire rains on the scene. Death and death.

I think of writing and writers when recalling the shootout. Writing is hard work. Many obstacles and setbacks litter the attempt to perfect the skill. To begin, persist, and improve, writers have to develop courage and not so much recklessness as a sense of plunging ahead in the dark. They need to develop that "hard bark." Although it might sometimes feel like it, writing isn't "hell," and, literally, it won't will kill you. Figuratively? That's another matter.

I say these things not to discourage you but to level with you, a feature I maintain in this book. *Write It Real* could "sugarcoat" its guidelines and insights, which is what many instructors and guide books do. However, I have too much respect for writers of all abilities. As long as they remain serious about improving this vital skill, they have my pledge to keep it "real." I'll spill the secrets learned over a lifetime, the ones that actually work *on the page*.

Writers usually work alone. Their work faces criticism, constructive and otherwise. Rejection comes frequently. Get used to it. Your situation as a developing writer resembles that of an aspirant monk. In Buddhism, the prospective acolyte knocks on the monastery door. The roshi (master) answers holding a stick. Instead of greeting the applicant, the roshi strikes him and yells at the visitor to go away. If the applicant returns, it shows "true willingness" and the applicant receives welcome. The stick is the test of the applicant's determination to persevere against all difficulty.

I wrote this book to share insights learned since my professional career with words began just before Memorial Day weekend 1975, when I joined the newsroom at the *Syracuse Post-Standard*, one of the New York State's largest dailies. Since then, I have made my living with words — writing, teaching, and speaking them. Along the way, I've gained insights into this vexing, mysterious, complex, and profoundly simple skill. This book shares what I've learned in the hopes that it can profit writers at all levels of ability.

My time teaching in college classrooms, on the "other side of the desk," gave me the chance over many years to figure out the best way to help developing writers. Thousands of students and millions of published words later, I have refined my understanding of how writing works. This book presents most of what I have learned and practiced over the decades.

Learning to write with polish and craft can be truly great with its satisfactions and rewards, be they psychic, monetary, or both. The monk aims for enlightenment. The writer aims for clarity. When he achieves enlightenment, the monk can't put it into words. When a writer achieves the breakthrough, however, they *can* put it into words, which is the point in the first place.

Write It Real focuses on the practical aspects of this vital skill—and it is just that, a skill requiring constant practice. I'm not a linguist, an academic, or a communication theorist. While I am interested in the theoretical underpinnings of writing, I'm more focused on the actuality of the *doing*.

My book will help anyone serious about improving their ability to write effectively, be it for school, work, or any other situation that requires a message to be "put into words." If that's you, you've come to the right place. *Write It Real* isn't grammar-heavy. It doesn't waste time on too much theory. Contrarily, it shares pragmatic strategies, techniques, and tips designed to help your writing match your thinking so that your work represents you at your best and most articulate.

This isn't a handbook, though it is a book you will want to keep at hand. It can provide a "safety net" to have by your side whenever you write. Some of you might be professional writers. Some perhaps about to enter a college composition class for the first time, nervous as all get-out. Maybe you need to write for work, or perhaps you write with aspirations that involve personal fulfillment. Fortunately, the elements of good writing reduce to a few classic principles common to all scribes. These elements form the basis of *Write It Real*.

I hope my book provides you with the tools to take your writing to a higher level. Remember, there's no ceiling. You can take your writing to the stars—and keep going.

Best of luck.

—Dan Valenti
July 30, 2022

Preface

This book began in 1973 when something astounding occurred.

I was in my junior year at Union College in Schenectady, NY, majoring in English. Having racked up departmental honors for my work, I toyed with becoming a writer. One day after class, Prof. Sam Ullman said, "You have the goods." He encouraged me and told me I could turn my writing from "a procession into a profession." I asked him what he meant. Prof. Ullman said my work could become a path on which I could journey ahead into the professional ranks. That floored me. Dan Valenti? Good enough to become "a Writer?"

The second piece fell into place during lit courses at the same school. It occurred to me how many writers had a journalism background: Bram Stoker, Edgar Allen Poe, Charles Dickens, Theodore Dreiser, Ambrose Bierce, George Orwell, H.L. Mencken, Truman Capote, Ernest Hemingway, Stephen Crane, and countless others. Then it hit me. Become a writer—I could think of nothing I wanted more.

A career path emerged. After receiving my BA in English at Union, the Newhouse School of Syracuse University, America's finest journalism school, accepted me for its graduate program. I earned my MA in newspaper journalism six months after I began work as an actual news hawk at the city's morning daily. The six-month intersection of academics and full-time newspapering made me the busiest man in the news business. I chose newspapers as a way to break into the writing business. There are other avenues: T.S. Eliot was a banker, and Wallace

Stevens, an insurance executive. Hart Crane and Kurt Vonnegut started writing advertising and marketing copy.

The point is that everyone begins some place, irrespective of their ambitions. After five years in daily newspapers, I realized I was ready. I took the leap, hung a shingle, became a writer, and haven't looked back since.

My goal wasn't to be a starving artist. I wanted to write for a living. I was also willing to dive in head first, remembering a piece of advice from Hart Crane that to become competent, a writer must become "drenched in words." I drenched myself, hustling assignments and winning confidence of people to pay for my skills. Since then, I have been on an endless quest to improve. That doesn't stop, and it won't (at least it shouldn't) for you.

Then along came the pandemic. Along with the rest of the world, I retreated into the Fortress of Solitude, only I was determined to put the downtime to good use. That's when I began this book.

The words gushed in a torrent. The keyboard acted as if separate from my volition. As a writer, you've probably known the thrill of "being in the zone." Well, I got in the zone. I realized this book had been percolating in me for decades. It only needed the outlet provided by time.

You now possess the end result.

Writing may be your passion. It may not be. Experience tells me that most of you shrink from writing if you don't hate it outright. This book is for both categories, with a special nod to those who rate writing up there with a root canal, scrubbing toilets, and sleeping in a swamp.

Relax. I've got you covered. You only need one prerequisite. You have to care enough about your work that you're willing to dig in for the long haul.

With that, let me pronounce you "ready."

Now get to work.

Acknowledgments

I'll keep it brief. I dislike works that acknowledge everyone in the author's life since birth, like the winners do in those hideous Oscar speeches. Inevitably you leave someone out, and too many names are there for political reasons.

That said, some people deserve recognition. First hat-tip to the instructors and editors over the years who taught me the basics and instilled a work ethic: Venerini Sisters Loretta Ciccarelli and Rosa Guiliano; professors Mary Lawrence, Len McCue, Molly Leonard, Win Piper, Frank Gado, Sam Ullman, Richard Peck, Burt Marvin, and Lee Becker; and editors Rollie Allen, George Carr, George Swayze, Paul Kocak, Mark Murphy, Gary Van Dusen, and Lou Rappaport.

Second, a derby nod to Peter Lang Publishing. Acquisitions editor Dani Green couldn't have been more accommodating and supportive. Same goes for Jackie Pavlovic, who headed production. And gratitude to the peer reviewers. They offered vital input and direction.

Third, wife Lisa. She did her art. I wrote this book.

Finally, I acknowledge my readers. Thanks for completing my creative task.

List of Abbreviations

BME	Beginning, middle, and ending
CI	Controlling idea
CS	Comma splice
DW	Deadwood
FRAG	Sentence fragment
FS	Fused sentence
TS	Topic sentence

CHAPTER ONE

Get Ready to Write

What do you think? Is the decision to write versus the resolution to become a writer a distinction without a difference or are they two different species?

The first case applies to anyone who, for whatever reason, needs to put pen to paper or keyboard to screen using words as the conveyers of ideas and insights. This includes writing for your job; term papers for school; sending a letter, e-mail, or text to someone; leaving instructions for a house sitter; writing a memo; and countless other tasks.

The second describes a person who elevates their use of a skill bordering on magic—the act and art of communication—as a means to a profession. If you can't make a living at it, does it count? Will you still be a writer? That's for you to decide. In any case, you want your words to provide the best chance possible for acceptance and perhaps even sales. Trust me: The greatest feeling in the world is getting paid to write. Second best is the sense of fulfillment that comes from being able to write at an elite level.

Fortunately, this book can help both the everyday writer and the professional writer for the simple reason that both require utility and nearly to the same degree. If your techniques, strategies, and style won't work on the page, then why bother, because they won't work upon submission. No one wants their writing to become the answer to the question: "What's the use?"

I've written this book for writers who want to improve what they do *on the page*, where effective communication and the conveyance of pure thought finds its pragmatic crucible. Either you succeed or you don't. In that sense, effective writing constitutes a zero-sum game. Yes, readers are that cruel. They'll dump you in a second.

Within that starkness of "do or don't" exists a murky, muddy, middle ground where your reader (the most important person in a scribe's universe) can more or less fathom your message, and only after much struggling. For ordinary writing, that may be enough. For example, your boss reads the report on yesterday's sales meeting and gets a vague idea of what transpired. The professional writer trying to make a living doesn't have it that easy. The pro finds in their reader the severest of all critics, a person who reads for enjoyment or enlightenment and is willing to back that up by putting money on the line, which is what they do when they buy your work.

In *Write It Real*, I'm aiming high but not unrealistically. I'll share the "secrets" of writing that will take you out of the no man's land of indecisive prose and into clear and effective communication. Our exploration will include a detailed look at the parameters that affect nonfiction writing—expository prose—including different rhetorical strategies, planning, drafting, revision, grammar, and many other factors. While certain principles hold true for any writing, and any writer can profit from this book, poetry and fiction belong to a different species, even a different genus.

My intended audience is the nonfiction writer. Poets, novelists, and short-story writers are welcome, of course, but primarily I'll share the techniques and tips that help nonfiction scribes achieve greater clarity and precision in their work. Fiction and especially poetry allow enormous leeway in structure, chronology, invention, and depiction, even in worlds and states of mind and being that don't exist except in the figurative sense. When novelists write about events, characters, times, and worlds that don't exist except in their imaginations, who can argue with what's depicted? Try doing that, however, when writing up a set of instructions on how to design an ad campaign or writing on deadline the game story for a hockey match, and see how far that gets you.

In contrast to their poetic and novelistic kin, nonfiction writers deal almost exclusively in description and narrative that reflect case actualities. Of course, there's still plenty of room to roam in terms of creativity. For instance, the use of subjective techniques such as figurative language, simile, and metaphor has a decided place in nonfiction. Moreover, for decades, certain techniques of fiction (speculative dialogue, interior monologue, foreshadowing) have found a place in nonfiction, as anyone familiar with the work of Tom Wolfe, Gay Talese, Hunter Thompson,

Norman Mailer, and Gore Vidal can attest. Nonetheless, linguistic adherence to actual occurrence and identifiable circumstance has greater urgency, rising to predominance in nonfiction.

In writing up a report for work, your boss or manager isn't looking for great literature. They want the story and the facts conveyed with prosaic expertise, assurance, certainty, and with as little guesswork as possible. Clarity. Above all, blessed clarity.

In reading and using this book, trust me and most of all trust yourself: You can achieve your writing goals. This book will show you how.

Plan First, Compose After—Like Yogi

Where to begin?

Once in the middle of a batting slump, baseball great Yogi Berra sought advice from various hitters and coaches. Each didn't hesitate with generous amounts of advice and instant fixes.

"Open your hips sooner."

"Shift your weight to the front foot."

"Don't chase pitches out of the strike zone."

The well-meaning tips had Yogi's head in a Bronx fog. Finally, an exasperated Berra blurted out, "I can't hit and think at the same time."

Same applies to writing. You can't think and write at the same time, at least not until you've had about a million published words under your belt, then perhaps. What does this mean? How can you not think while you write?

Strictly speaking, of course, as you put words on the page, your mind has to be engaged. Yes, that's thinking. There's a big "however" in this, however. The bulk of your planning has to be behind you by the time you address the blank page and begin your first draft. I have seen too many developing writers attempting to tackle an assignment with a haste that makes "hurry" look slow, placing words on the page before they are ready. That's not writing. That's scribbling, a "back-in" approach to writing that rarely, if ever, works, especially for the developing writer.

At the outset, I want to clear up one important point. This isn't a textbook on usage or grammar. Once you've made it as far as a college-level writing course or as a non-student learner having decided to make a serious attempt at improving your skills and possibly becoming a professional, I have to take your basic knowledge of grammar for granted. This doesn't mean you can cite verse and chapter or tell me the difference between a compound sentence and a compound adjective. It simply means that you should have a fundamental understanding of how writing functions syntactically and how "grammatical glue" holds the words and paragraphs together.

Consequently, I won't be taking up large amounts of time or space on the finer points of grammar. Those devils can be found only in the details. What I will do in a later chapter is walk you through some of the technical obstacles that trip up many writers. I promise to make it painless and informative. And I'll seal the one simple principle that guides every grammatical issue you might have, which is simply the ability to immediately recognize subject and verbs.

If you feel you need to brush up on your dangling particles and eight parts of speech in a more fundamental way, there are plenty of good handbooks to help you. For a reliable, easy-to-use handbook, I can recommend *The Little, Brown Compact Handbook* by Jane Aaron or *Easy Writer* by Andrea Lunsford. Then relax. Go to work but realize it's not important that you can define grammatical terms and elements as long as you can correctly use them. I can tell you right off the bat that you probably need a refresher on punctuation, especially comma usage. I'll give you that refresher in Chapter Seven.

Along the way, I'll share what I call "Swing Thoughts."

If you went to a golf pro for help on your swing, they would take you to a driving range, put a 7-iron in your hand, and watch you hit a bucket of balls. They would make observations, take notes, and not overwhelm you with information. Rather, they would boil each lesson down to one or two "Swing Thoughts" to take with you the next time you played golf. It would be something like, "Concentrate on keeping your head down when you drive or hit from the fairway" or "Slow your backswing." That's the approach I take here. I'll leave you with Swing Thoughts you can apply to your writing. Here's our first:

SWING THOUGHT NO. 1—YOU MUST BE *READY* TO *WRITE*

—Writing is a strategic process. You must be mentally ready with total focus.
—Before your first draft, get your thinking and planning out of the way.
—Realize that your current ability does not reflect your ultimate potential.

Later, we'll get into the specifics of how to know if you're ready to write plus the many details that will advance your writing, a process that you've already begun with this book. You're on your way and can allow yourself to proceed with confidence.

Before getting into that, let me share a few more general thoughts about being mentally ready for the task. This will help you avoid the "Yogi-ism" of too much thinking while in the act itself.

To write effective prose, every writer without exception brings to the page their existing ability level. This is not their talent capacity; a writer's present ability is never equal to their potential or talent ceiling. Writing is like striving for sainthood. There will always be room for improvement, no matter how close you get to perfection.

Each writer possesses a different level of existing skill we can call "X." As you may recall, in algebra "X" stands for the unknown. On that first day of a composition course, for example, the professor doesn't know the "X" for each person in the room. Similarly for you, the reader of this book, I don't know your writing "X."

This shapes our mutual goal: To help take your "X" and boost it to at least "X + 1." That's my minimum expectation, and "+1" is attainable by everyone seriously interested in improvement. If this book leads you to at least "X + 1," then you got your money's worth.

Actually, there's no limit to how much you can dramatically improve. I've seen it happen, and I've had students who went on to become published writers. It occurred that way with me. I majored in English, then got a graduate degree in journalism. It's now more than six million published words later.

There's nothing that prevents a self-starter with determination to take what they learn in this book and apply it on their own, continuing what we started and in effect customizing an individualized writing course. Along the way, you might discover abilities you never suspected you had and an enjoyment from writing you didn't know existed. At that point, writing becomes less of a chore. This will happen, however, only if you "flip the switch" that removes hesitancy and allows you to dive fearlessly into your work with total commitment. That spells the difference between a serious writer and a dabbler.

The Challenge of "How"

The range of skill levels among students as they sit in the classroom on that terrifying first day of the semester or in the intrepid person determined to improve their prose runs from "overwhelmed" to "accomplished" and everything in between. This brings us to the greatest challenge in teaching the "how" of writing. How can any one set of instructions work for everyone, given that each person has different strengths and weaknesses and all have discrete needs? It's a tough situation, but the problem has more than a response. It has a solution. That's what I present in this book. Linguistic skill isn't guesswork or voodoo. It's not mysterious, though it can produce dazzling results bordering on magic and mystery.

I'll give you "how" in straightforward terms, easy to follow, light on technical jargon, and heavy on showing you what works *on the page*. That's where you measure a good writing course. What can you produce *on the page*? Can you write as opposed to just memorize writing principles?

I've taught in college English departments where some composition instructors had never published a word. They weren't writers. They were pedagogues who tended to teach theory, leading to all sorts of useless busy work for their students. The assignments might include rote exercises in grammar from cookie-cutter worksheets or quizzes that tested how well students could regurgitate a classroom lecture in a blue book. That's all well and good, but it usually doesn't help improve writing. Even professional writing instruction for non-student learners often falls into this abstract "theory" trap.

It's true that any effective system has theory behind it, and writing's no different. For serious writers, however, practice precedes theory. Do first, theorize much later. Writing is concurrent; theory is after the fact. The "academic" approach alone isn't good enough. Developing writers need to be exposed to writing from the inside and armed with tools and strategies that have a practical benefit on the outside. Only someone who regularly writes, both the pragmatic and professional writer, can do that.

When I used to tell my students "I'm a writer," some nervously expected I would judge them by professional standards. After a few weeks into the semester, though, they'd learned the opposite. I would meet writers at their level, whatever it might be, approaching them more as colleagues than as students.

You can *Google* search my name and get a sense of my career. It has included five years of daily newspapering and more than 40 years as a writer and author (probably 4,000 newspaper columns, 17 books authored counting editions, 7 books edited, plus countless magazine and Internet articles, press releases, speeches, radio and TV scripts, ad copy, reports, and more). In addition, I have hosted and produced more than 4,000 editions of an award-winning radio talk show in the morning-drive slot for a commercial AM-FM station. Topping off a career with the English language, for almost 30 years I taught as an adjunct professor in the English departments of two colleges. Courses taught included mass communications, expository writing, composition, journalism, business writing, poetry, film, and even a course on America's "The Sixties." I share this information to boost your trust in my methods. You are in good hands.

However, I have never thought of myself as The Expert, coming from on high and teaching down to the lowly learners. I had been in classes like that as an undergraduate and didn't like it, vowing that if I ever got "on the other side of the desk," I'd never treat writers that way. My notion of good instruction comes from my desire to mutually explore the topic of writing as a fellow learner with my students and not from the position of the expert dealing with the tyro and doling out wisdom the old-school way.

We will explore the topic as equals. Invariably, I end up learning as much as anyone. This book reflects that approach. It's as if we are fellow scientists engaged in a common experiment designed for mutual benefit and self-interest.

Assured Reliability

People sometimes ask me, "What do you do for a living?" I answer, "I exchange words for dollar bills." The pithy response describes my attitude toward writing that I began to develop as an undergrad English major at Union College, when I first got the idea of doing it for a living. Further guidance came from the likes of Edgar Allan Poe, Walt Whitman, Ambrose Bierce, Theodore Dreiser, Ernest Hemingway, H.L. Mencken, Truman Capote, Walter Lippmann, Westbrook Pegler, and the countless other American authors who got their start as journalists.

That took me to graduate school, where I got my master's degree from the S I. Newhouse School of Public Communications at Syracuse University. From there I went directly to the *Syracuse Post-Standard*, the city's morning daily, then to another metro daily, the *Wilkes-Barre Times Leader*. In those five newspaper years I learned more about writing, editing, and meeting deadlines than a lifetime's worth of study could have supplied. After that, I took a dive into the deep end of the pool, giving up a steady paycheck to become "a writer." My goal was to see my name on the cover of a book. I've had that pleasure.

I used to joke that I wanted to be able to look myself up in a library's indexing system in case I ever had an identity crisis. When my first published book came out in 1979, librarians indexed using the "card catalog." There it was, my name on that punched, ringed index card, in libraries across America.

The point is that I had a goal, defined it specifically, and pursued it. You can and should do the same. I would invite you now to write out your goals. What do you want to achieve with your writing? Maybe it's polishing a resume, getting a promotion, or even personal fulfillment. Consider it your first "assignment." Be specific.

As a guy who has made his living with words his entire professional life, I developed a system of teaching how to write, refining it to the point of "assured reliability." My system works. It's not infallible, of course, which reminds me of the old saw: "There are three never-fail rules for learning how to write. (PAUSE) Unfortunately, no one knows what they are."

While I can offer no guarantees, I can promise that if you commit to doing your part, which is to diligently apply what I share to the best of your abilities, you'll improve. As long as you don't quit, you'll find yourself making noticeable strides. Writing is a skill, after all, and the only way to improve a skill is that joke about getting to Carnegie Hall: practice, practice, practice.

My method relies on *specifics*, the tools and the tips upon which to build impressive writing. The prose you produce will show greater unity. Your writing will become clearer and more focused. It won't wander as much. It will engage readers as it has not done before. You'll learn how to overcome the so-called writer's block (surprise: there's no such thing). Your thinking, in turn, will become clearer. That will spill into your writing, and you will have put into motion a creative feedback loop.

Moreover, you'll learn how to plan and organize your thoughts into coherence with techniques particular to the nature of the writing assignment and within the context of your particular abilities. In this way, each of you can apply these teachings in a specific, case-applied manner. You and your writing colleagues—all writers, really—have the same destination, which is to improve, but each of you will end up there only after journeys as varied as are the participating travelers. To borrow from poet T.S. Eliot, after the long trip you'll arrive where you began and see the place for the first time.

Back to our first Swing Thought. Before you can begin to think about constructing a coherent, unified piece of prose, you must be *ready* to do it. You'd be shocked to learn how many developing and would-be writers are anything but ready. Without doubt, this explains most of the poor writing I've encountered.

Sitting at the keyboard without having prepared a plan is like buying the materials and beginning to build a house without a set of blueprints. Good luck. What started out to be a craftsman bungalow turns out to be an unfinished, rickety outhouse. You can't force good writing or jump-start excellence, nor can you forestall beginning an assignment until the night before it's due, start "writing" cold, and expect that your work will impress anyone. Try doing that to a book publisher or the editor of a magazine, newspaper, or blog. See how many more assignments you get. No. You'll then find making a shopping list was the apex of your career as a writer.

There used to be a wine commercial that had Orson Welles touting the tag line in his ocean-deep baritone: "Paul Mason will sell no wine before its time." Similarly, writers should not begin much less present no work "before its time."

That would be like picking unripe grapes as your feedstock. The vintage will be memorable but not for the reasons you want.

Writing effective prose is *a strategic process. You must properly prepare.* Skip any step of the process, and you will have zero chance of submitting your best work. You will flop. It would be like baking a cake but skipping the sugar or flour because you didn't have time to buy the ingredients or were just too lazy. Can you imagine what will come out of the oven?

Follow the process that I outline, however, and you will succeed. When applied with the proper steps, your writing will produce a solid result. Invariably. Each time. This frees you from cold sweat when your instructor presents a new writing assignment or the next time you sit at the keyboard looking to produce for the next meeting of your writers' group. You will be armed with a technique that does not fail and cannot, if you (a) learn it and (b) consistently apply it with no shortcuts.

Here's the truth, expressed in our next Swing Thought.

SWING THOUGHT NO. 2—WRITING IS HARD WORK

—Finished writing comes only after intense effort.
—Poor writing usually stems from lack of planning.
—Take responsibility by "owning your words."

Of course, you already know how difficult writing can be from earlier experiences with any kind of serious deadline writing. It's often why students often prevent taking composition for as long as possible, or when there's a job report needed by Tuesday morning, you dread starting and delay to Monday night. When you commit to write, realize that it's going to ask much more of your time and focus than sending a casual text of the "whassup" variety to a friend.

Producing good writing is nothing less than trying to pluck from your head an understanding of life and transferring it as accurately as you can onto paper or screen. Do it well, and you're like a magician who appears to be walking on water or levitating. Read George Orwell's classic essay "Shooting an Elephant" and see what I mean. Orwell makes the steamy slums of Moulmein, Burma come to life. You can almost see the devastation caused by a rogue elephant that tramples a guy, taking the skin off his back. You are "there" with Orwell when he realizes that the crowd of thousands expects him to shoot the now-calm animal. Do you think the writing just happened with Orwell casually skating away on the thick ice of gliding prose? No way. Like the magician obsessively practicing his levitation trick, he worked on it tirelessly through countless drafts.

Both good writers and expert magicians seem effortless in their work. As a member of the audience, you marvel at the prestidigitator's illusion. You don't see the dreary hours of practice spent perfecting the trick. Similarly, when you read something that you enjoy, you marvel at how the author has so "effortlessly" managed to convey feelings and expressions that connect with you, the reader, in a meaningful way. What you don't see is that same author sweating proverbial drops of blood at the keyboard, laboring to make the writing as good as it can be though revision after revision. Having written books with a typewriter, I can only offer thanks to IBM, Amstrad, Hewlett-Packard, Compaq, Dell, Microsoft, and Apple for computers and word-processing programs that don't involve retyping reams of pages. Back in the day, white-out could only cover so many sins. Compared to typewriters, computers have taken much of the drudge out of revision, eliminating that excuse (one that good writers never used).

Your readers only see the finished product. However, writers see the process from the inside, all the effort and toil put in beforehand, much of it laborious and challenging—what drives many would-be writers into mediocrity or away from words entirely.

It's Okay to Have Doubt

There's another reason why writing seems like pushing a boulder up a steep incline, Sisyphus-like. When you share your work with someone, you reveal a lot about yourself. How you use words and language, in speaking as well as writing, shows readers or listeners how you think, like providing a CAT scan of your mind. The written words expose you, letting others into your head, where they walk around the inside of how your thinking functions, much like patrons of an art gallery. They may not like the work. That can cause you doubts. The internal critic who lives inside each of us likes to magnify these doubts out of proportion and throw them at you as if you were sitting on the dunking chair of a carnival's water booth. That's fine, but only up to a point. Such inner qualms actually indicate you care about what you do. After that point, they suffocate the writer as efficiently as a serial killer.

No matter how mundane the topic, the words that you choose, the sequence in which you place them, the context within which they appear, all reveal something intimate about yourself. They provide evidence of how you think. Most people find that intimidating, almost as nerve-wracking as public speaking or a fear of heights. If that's you, don't despair. Know that most developing writers feel the same way. So do many published writers, who will often eschew interviews or speaking engagements because, having opened themselves up on the page, they now dread facing live, real-time scrutiny.

When you write, try not to focus on your feelings and allow yourself some slack. It's okay to feel the butterflies. It's not okay to beat yourself up. Also remember that fear can actually be a measure of how well you want to perform. Fear shows you care about your work. As the saying goes, fear is the dragon that guards your treasures. You can appease the dragon to access the treasures, because it's much more friendly than you realize.

Take comfort in the fact that you belong where you are as a writer. Honestly acknowledge your ability. If you didn't care, you wouldn't be reading this book. You've qualified to be where you find yourself. You've been through elementary-, middle-, and high-school writing and perhaps college English classes. You might even be a working stiff needing to get sharper with your emails, memos, and reports. If you've made it this far, you can do the rest.

Do you fear writing? Ask this of yourself and honestly answer. Such self-inquiry is a part of getting ready to write. If you have such trepidation, understand that fear has two causes. First, it's a sign of how seriously you take the skill that so many others overlook. To adapt a truism, those who *won't* write have no advantage over those who *can't* write. Moreover, those who do write by choice or assignment realize that judgment awaits in the form of a grade, a promotion, or a critic's review. Second, fear of writing often stems from not being properly taught how to write in those classes from your formal education. You may have been taught *about* writing, but that's not the same thing as actually doing it and lots of it, with proper guidance and meaningful feedback. You weren't shown how to discover the pleasure of reading or the immense creative satisfaction that comes from putting your own words to paper to say something new and unique.

This book gives you the *how*.

Comparing You to You and Only You

As you sit in the classroom on the first day of class or about to submit a job report, look around. It's easy for the internal critic to begin with the whispers: "Everyone else is ready, but I'm not" … "They're all better than me" … "What am I doing here?" and other such lies. In the same way, when you sit down to compose, you may tend to look at the work of other writers, published and successful, and think, "That's not me. I'll never be that good."

All serious writers at some point become aware of such thinking. When they find these shards of doubt piercing confidence like ballistic shrapnel, good writers immediately change their head space by realizing the futility of such comparisons. The point? Don't compare yourself with others. You'll always find someone who's better than you and someone who's not. Comparison then turns into a pointless mind game you play depending on whether you want to needlessly work yourself over or to artificially feel superior. *The only fair comparison a writer ever makes is to themselves.* Are you improving? Are you a better writer now than you were five weeks ago? These are the true indications of progress.

In this book, I will demystify the writing process and show you how to produce clear, readable prose *on demand.* If you follow these guidelines, you will produce writing that *communicates* your ideas clearly and concisely. Communication takes a message and sends it to a receiver through a channel or medium—in a writer's case, to the reader. On the surface, communication seems easy. Beneath the veneer, however, numerous factors can and do impede the message from getting through the way you intended. Anyone who's ever had a misunderstanding with a friend or loved one knows what I'm talking about. Effective communication proves deceptively difficult.

When you learn how to advance your writing skills, you will do nothing less than become a proficient communicator, and that's worth dollars and cents. Take any two candidates for a job or promotion with equal skills, and—politics aside—the more effective communicator wins the position every time.

Gain skills in writing, and you will find your mindset progressing from

* Declaration: I can't do this.
* Possibility: I don't think I can do this.
* Hope: I might be able to do this.
* Observation: I'm doing it.
* Accomplishment: I did it!

Congratulations, because at that point, you're a writer.

In Review

Here are the Swings Thoughts from Chapter One. Think about them. Ask yourself how they apply to the way you approach and execute writing assignments. Do this for all the Swing Thoughts in this book.

1. You must be ready to write.
2. Writing is hard work. You must commit to the heavy lifting.

Writing Prompts

At the end of each chapter, you'll find suggestions for writing assignments particular to the chapter. Think of them as workouts, similar to how you would stretch out, exercise, and practice before going into the actual game. A musician tunes up and runs scales before the gig, and a soldier trains before going into combat. Same with writers, who seek as many chances to practice as their schedules allow.

Respond to the following. Word count: No greater than 300 words. Be specific.

1. What you do you see as your greatest strengths as a writer?
2. What are your greatest weaknesses?
3. What are your realistic writing goals?

Suggestions for Reading

1. Stephen King, *On Writing: A Memoir of a Craft*—The prolific novelist shares his experiences trying to break into print, offering tips and advice that can help any serious writer.
2. Roy Peter Clark, *Writing Tools: Essential Writing Strategies*—A pragmatic approach to learning the craft, summed up well by Peters' assertion that writers "need tools, not rules."
3. Benjamin Dryer, *Dreyer's English*—Writing's dos and don'ts are presented in a humorous way, boiled down to the essentials.

CHAPTER TWO

Own Your Words

Once you've produced good writing, especially on deadline, you establish a pattern that soon becomes a reliable track record. I can remember many times receiving an assignment that at first glance seemed well beyond my capabilities. For instance, a *Fortune* Three company once hired me to produce a comprehensive design guide for architects and designers working with engineering thermoplastics.

What did I know about plastics other than that famous scene in *The Graduate*? Then I took stock of the many times I'd written about topics of which I had little experience: virtual reality, agriculture, flying, construction, health care, packaging, architecture, politics, history. Each time I developed the mastery needed to produce. No one was more dogged with research. If I needed to talk to the experts, no one tracked them down more resolutely. I acknowledged what I didn't know and went about educating myself.

This underlines one of the great ironies about writing. Those with an inflated view of their abilities often can't put one coherent sentence together. They've just been passed through middle school, high school, and college not knowing what they don't know and riding on the high tide of grade inflation. On the other hand, those who have a healthy, humble perspective about their words can usually produce good work, although they are rarely, if ever, satisfied.

There are canyons-full of lamentations from famous writers who talk about their difficulties and doubts. Ernest Hemingway, J.K. Rowling, Agatha Christie,

Charles Bukowski, Henry Miller, F. Scott Fitzgerald, George Bernard Shaw, and so many others were told to forget about writing in school or later. Publishing is full of the seemingly endless rejections that authors had to endure before hitting their stride and tasting success. Some examples:

— Kate DiCamillo was rejected 473 times before finding a publisher for *Because of Winn-Dixie*.
— Hundreds of publishers turned down Alex Haley's *Roots* before it became an international bestseller and turned into an epic TV miniseries.
— James Joyce's *Ulysses*, voted in a millennial poll the greatest book of the 20th century, saw many publishers turn it down because of its alleged gibberish and obscenity.
— *Lord of the Flies* by William Golding had the door slammed more than 20 times.
— Stephen King's first novel, *Carrie*, got rejected 30 times.
— *Zen and the Art of Motorcycle Maintenance* by Robert Pirsig ran the gauntlet 121 times prior to making it to bestseller status.

The lesson here? NGU.

"N" = Never. "G" = Give. "U" = Up.

Never Give Up. I like to remind myself of these examples whenever I'm struggling to get something into publication.

Each of these writers retained at least a fleck of doubt and most at some point lost heart—but they never quit. Some had enough fear and loathing to fill a dump truck with rejection slips. Each person, though, knew the truth. Bestselling author Haruki Murakami once remarked, "There is no such thing as perfect writing, just as there is no such thing as perfect despair." The two are related.

Give Your Writing the Respect It Deserves

Even from your initial efforts, *own your words*. Take your writing seriously. Don't slapdash writing or give it lip service. That will signal to readers that you don't care and invite them to wonder why *they* should. Rushed, hurried writing begun shortly before deadline also makes it impossible to submit your best work. Nothing makes a reader bail faster or an editor search for the circular file faster than sloppy prose.

Own your words. Never be defensive about your output, irrespective of its merits. If you've put in an honest effort including full-force revision, you never need apologize. If you do hand in a dog, take responsibility. Don't make excuses.

Instead, make an effort to better your work next time out, trying to learn from your mistakes. Every time you write, you can learn and improve.

The mature writer harkens back to Murakami's observation. Unless you're pitcher Don Larsen on October 8, 1956 at Yankee Stadium (look it up), perfection isn't possible—but it's always the goal. Know that you can get closer and closer to it. With each new work, with each revision of the same work, you can inch nearer to impeccability. Same as with any skill, the more you practice with a guiding hand to help, the faster you will advance and progress. This book provides that helping hand.

Now are you sitting down?

Good.

Take a deep breath.

Ready? Here it comes.

Writing is a creative activity.

What? Spare you the obvious?

Not a chance.

Every time you compose, you give birth to a small piece of knowledge that prior to your bringing it into being did not exist in the world, ever. You need to approach your writing with this sense of wonder, creation, and discovery. Writing borders on the sacred, if I am not being too profane in the declaration. Believe that *you have something to say and that it's worth saying*, experiences worth sharing, and insights worth expressing. From the moment you took your first breath to where you are now, you have weathered all manner of success and failure. You've experienced exhilarating highs and crushing lows. It's all subject material. Believe also that there are readers who will want to learn your views on various topics. They are there, those curious souls who can't read enough whether for vicarious entertainment or to gain information and acquire knowledge.

When you begin to improve as a writer and your confidence grows, a beneficial snowball effect occurs. More confidence equals better writing which produces more assurance, more positivity, and improved writing.

You will also notice a benefit to your reading. As you improve as a writer, your reading becomes more efficient, and so does retention. I often have been asked: "How can I speed up my reading?" The question bugs me because it's the wrong question. Reading isn't a matter of speed but of grasp. You should never read at a speed faster than your ability to comprehend. Yes, there are tricks that cut corners such as skimming paragraphs by reading only the topic sentence, but such gimmicks in the long run rob you of information, nuance, and enjoyment.

When I did talk radio, guests would often include authors. The author's publicity people would send me the book. Did I read every one? No. It couldn't be done with the schedule I had, so I'd read the jacket blurbs and maybe scanned a couple chapters that seemed most important. For talk radio that approach works. For writing assignments and research, avoid at all costs.

Chances are if you're serious about improving your prose, you're already a reader, maybe even a voracious one. Those two skills produce a perfect yin–yang circle. Without exception, every good writer I've known or know of were and are readers. Likewise, most excellent readers can usually handle themselves when dishing out the words. Each time you read, you absorb something of not just the words and ideas but also *how* the words convey the ideas. It stands to reason, then, that reading more, especially reading more challenging material than you would typically tackle, transfers to your writing. Be convinced, though, that everything you read, even if it's the back of the cereal box at breakfast, produces a positive effect on your writing. Good writing satisfies you. Great writing awes you. Poor writing teaches you what to avoid in your own work.

Reading offers exposure to many different writing styles with different levels of complexity. You should make a conscious effort to increase not just the volume of your reading but also the scope and difficulty. Venture out into unfamiliar topics and writers you have never read. I suggest getting a prose anthology. I can recommend *The Blair Reader* (Laurie Kirszner and Stephen Mandell, eds.) and *Prose Models* (Gerald Levin, ed.).

Readers literally retain every word if not consciously then subconsciously deep within the brain, which, as neurological research shows, forgets nothing. As you read, little gears turn in your head—you won't even be aware—storing information. At some point, if you write enough words, traces of those long-digested words will incorporate themselves into your work helping you to develop a style, that is, a unique literary fingerprint.

As your writing develops, your literary instincts will improve, and you will begin to carve out a signature style. The more you read, the more you will begin to pick up clues about how and why the material holds together as well as it does. You will be like a proverbial sponge, absorbing some of everything you read. Invariably, this has a beneficial effect on your own work.

You Have a Lot to Say

If you're like the many to whom I've taught writing, you might be thinking, "My life is boring. I having nothing to say." It's a common assumption that continually surprises me.

I don't buy a drop of it.

I think of a remark made by writer Dorothy Parker during an Algonquin Roundtable session—that nothing bad ever happens to a writer. Why? It's not because writers don't have the same problems as anyone else. They do. It's not because they live magical, protected lives. They don't.

Nothing bad ever happens to a writer because everything and anything can be a fit subject for prose treatment. In fact, the worst moments of your life often provide the best material. Your times of actual failure, deep sadness, and intense loss can pack more emotion than the most melodramatic fiction. Think of the accounts of war, emotional distress, grief, and loss left by memoir writers over the years. Conflict drives stories and stories interest people. If that weren't true, you would have never heard of Harry Potter.

Your life is too boring? *Au contraire.*

You have lived through many amazing experiences. If you're like most everyone, you've experienced moments of not only exhilaration and triumph (scoring the winning TD in the high school Turkey Bowl) but also depression and sorrow (the death of a loved one or the horror of addiction). You don't get old enough to be in college or the workplace without having undergone many ups and down. Think also (and especially) of the so-called ordinary events of day-to-day life. These happenings often hide the material for the most amazing writing topics. I think, for example, of an essay by Garrison Keillor called "Hoppers."

In "Hoppers," Keillor finds himself standing at the corner of 7th Avenue and 23rd Street in New York City shortly after a fire hydrant has been flushed. The gush creates a huge puddle at the corner, one that pedestrians have to negotiate. Keillor describes how different people handle the task. Men and women, tall and short, stout and skinny, all employ different strategies and techniques. In the time it took for Keillor to watch this parade of puddle jumpers, probably hundreds of people saw the same thing, except he was the only one who lifted this quotidian experience out of the "ordinary" and into something sublime, a commentary on the quirks of human experience. Standup comics do this all the time, noting the ironies to be found in the oft-confounding situations of daily life. Yes, writing can do that. To paraphrase our good friend Yogi Berra again, you can see a lot just by observing. Good writers get much of their material this way. Simply look at the grand carousel of life that spins around each day. You'll find plenty to write about, way more material than you can use. Writers often keep journals or notebooks to take shorthand describing these little kernels or seeds for potential future work.

Here's another example of employing the "every day" as material.

When I was a boy, I went to summer camp, where I learned how to swim. I did well with freestyle and the various strokes, but the final obstacle threw me. To get my certificate, I had to dive into Richmond Pond off the high tower—12 feet tall but it looked like 1,200. When the day of the dive came, I felt trepidation from the pterodactyls in my stomach flying out of formation. Then I remembered something my dad told me: "Stop and think." In other words, pause, take a deep breath, and center yourself. The advice worked. I climbed the tower ladder, stood on the platform, and stepped off. When I popped to the surface, I let out a scream of happiness and joy.

An ordinary event, right? Routine. No big deal. But this minor event in the life of a lad gave me a lot of rich material with which to work. You have had countless such life lessons: Your first flame (Tom Wolfe's essay "A Sunday Kind of Love"), a fondly remembered family car (W.S. Merwin's essay "The Buick"), a favorite vacation spot (E.B. White's all-time classic, "Once More to the Lake"), a work experience (Gary Soto's "One Last Time"). These types of events and interactions happen every day. You only need to be on the lookout. That's what the Zen masters have been advising all along: Develop awareness. Wake up. Don't sleep.

Ho-hum situations will come in handy for assignments where you have to draw from personal experience or invent the topic. Other writing jobs pose no such problem. They will be assigned, specific, directed, and limited, as happens in classrooms, assignments from editors, writers' groups, and at work. When you're hard up for something to write about, however, the material can only be limited by a lack of imagination or a refusal to actually look.

One of my favorite warm-up exercises used to be composing a description of the immediate surroundings such as the backyard, the architecture of a building, or conveying the look and design of a fast-food wrapper—shape, color, ad copy along with speculations on why the company chose that particular design and layout. One of my favorites of these self-assigned exercises was describing a tea bag dipping into hot water. I likened it to a ship sinking, noting how the orange-colored streams lazily fingered out like leaking oil and oozing gas. When the saturated bag sank to the bottom of the cup, it was the "ship" going down. Taking the tea bag out of the water was the salvage crew at work.

You have plenty of material—now, this second—from the life you've already lived and through the common sense you have that enables you to do research. That's the other way to find material. You can't know everything. In fact, if you're like most people, your expertise has strict limits. Someone who flies an F-16 fighter jet for a living can probably tell you everything you would ever want to know about flying that viper, but could they tell you how to throw a curveball? A machinist knows the last details about threading a screw, but ask about a tax question and you might get the thousand-yard stare. The point is that you must trust that you have or can find way more than enough material about which to write.

You've Already Accomplished Your Greatest Achievement

Actually, you can relax knowing you have it licked. That's because you have already accomplished the most difficult intellectual challenge of your life. If you go on to discover a cure for cancer, if you come up with the quantum equations for a viable Theory of Everything, you still will not have equaled something you have already done. It involves language.

What am I talking about?

Learning to speak.

For nine months you lived in a prenatal paradise comfortably and safely floating weightless in body-temperature amniotic fluid. You existed in dreamy bliss doing the backstroke, nourished through the umbilical cord. Then suddenly you found yourself on the move. You were pushed out screaming and fighting only to find yourself in a strange, crowded room with blinding lights blazing overhead, except you had no conception of "room" or "lights" or "other people." Talk about the Twilight Zone. Masked, gowned beings stood around. One slapped you on the butt. You got a quick bath, someone snipped the cord, and from then on you were let loose. You went home.

Yet within two years of that bewildering experience, from scratch, you had learned how to speak having done most of the work on your own. You had to learn not just a new language but language itself, from conceptual and intellectual ground zero, and you did it.

How did you know where to begin? Have you ever thought about that? At birth and for the first few months, you couldn't even form conceptual thoughts. You had no ideational framework upon which you could rely and couldn't form abstract thoughts. Your bodily wants and needs produced cries and screams at which you made your first connection between utterance and gratification. Not a promising start, yet you plowed ahead undaunted.

Gradually, by observation, experiment, and experience—with a valuable assist from parents, siblings, aunts, uncles, neighbors, friends, and other helpers—you taught yourself how to speak. You managed to figure out how to operate English, one of the most complicated languages on earth. You were on your way to where you find yourself now, capable of attempting sophisticated, challenging writing assignments with a desire to improve your growing handling of prose.

Writing at Will

There's no more important skill a writer can develop than that of producing at will, what I call "deliberate writing." How do you learn to write at will? That's what this book shall reveal in a simple-to-follow, jargon-free set of instructions and guidelines.

What does "writing at will" mean?

Think of professional athletes. Through constant training, practice, and refinement of technique, they learn about both the physical and mental aspects of the skill, be it football, baseball, hockey, basketball, skiing, tennis, biking, swimming, or chess. Not matter the sport, they all had to develop muscle memory in the body and resolution of mind in the determination to perform, especially in and through the boredom and rigors of training and practice. For the writer and the chess master, the physical aspects, of course, are of less concern, although it helps enormously to stay in shape. The conceptual aspects of writing, however, also must be considered. A writer lives a life of the mind irrespective of whether they do it for a living or have to occasionally write to fulfill an assignment. "Writing at will" embraces this fact.

Writing starts with a resolution to begin, and for a serious writer, beginning implies a middle and an ending. This gets at the *writer's attitude* before the first word is put down on the screen or the page. You must realize that the *decision* to write lies entirely within your power to command. You don't have to "feel" like writing. In fact, feeling plays no part. There's beauty in this and a reason for confidence because it frees you from waiting around for inspiration. If you had to wait for the muse to visit every time you had to write, not much would ever get written and libraries, if built at all, could fit inside garden sheds.

To write at will reflects the writer's attitude toward performing the skill, much like the athlete. To write at will is an ethic—a philosophical perspective that imparts meaning and value even before the first word is written. Having this knowledge in hand often makes all the difference between a serious writer and a dilettante, someone who can get the job done versus someone with a passing interest who doesn't have the desire to see it through.

Unlike history, biology, art history, or math courses, writing doesn't involve mastering a specific body of knowledge. In learning to improve your writing, you're learning a higher level of a *skill* you already possess to some degree, which means that you "go Carnegie Hall," that is, practice, more practice, and still more practice. I can't tell you how many pages and notebooks I filled in college and long after trying to perfect my prose and poetry. I would invent assignments. One was to write in the style of different authors, from the sparse directness of Hemingway to the labyrinthian convolutions of Faulkner or Wolfe. I wrote poetry in many different forms—sonnets, couplets, triolets, haikus, epics, epigrams. Daily I made myself write. I kept journals with prose, poetry, and fiction. At some point, my brain developed a "muscle memory" for writing. The key point is that it took no extraordinary talent, just persistence and a desire to improve. I had learned to "write at will." So can you.

This leads to our third Swing Thought:

SWING THOUGHT NO. 3—THE ONLY WAY YOU CAN PERFECT A SKILL IS TO PRACTICE IT. *WRITING IS A SKILL.*

—Be sure to write every day.
—Invent writing assignments with different styles, including prose, poetry, and fiction.
—Keep at it. Accomplishment accrues with and through hard work and effort.

If you're learning how to act, you will rehearse and perform in many scenes involving different genres (comedy, tragedy, drama, farce, soliloquies). If you're learning how to drive a car with a standard transmission, you go to an empty lot and simulate different traffic conditions (parking, braking, shifting, etc.). You make mistakes, grinding the clutch, pumping the brakes too hard, stalling on the uphill, and with each failure you learn something and apply it to your next attempt. Similarly, if you're trying to improve as a writer, you will write as much as possible under different conditions. Combined with substantial reading, you will begin to develop an ear and an instinct for what works on the page—and what doesn't.

That's what you do in a writing course. Practice. Colleges and universities set aside Composition I and II expressly so students can practice writing expository prose. Composition isn't an adjunct as it is for other courses, where you write to demonstrate what you've learned studying particular disciplines. In a comp course, you write for writing's sake. Writing *is* the discipline and the course core. The good news is that you don't have to take a formal writing course to get the experience. With a book like this, you can design a course for yourself that addresses your particular needs. A good handbook will help.

Let me recommend my three favorite handbooks:

—*The Little, Brown Compact Handbook* by Jane Aaron
—*Easy Writer* by Andrea Lunsford

—*The Elements of Style* by William Strunk and E.B. White (the classic in the field).

Deliberate writing occurs when the writer learns to avoid the misconceptions about what it takes to put pen to paper or fingers to keyboard. Often, for example, the developing writer mistakenly thinks inspiration must be present to produce serviceable prose. We've all had moments when we begin to compose and the muse takes over. The writing flows effortlessly, expressing exactly what you want to say. You feel as if you've channeled a higher power. You're "in the zone." As you probably know from experience, however, these muse-filled moments arrive far too infrequently and unreliably to suit the needs of a serious writer.

Here we arrive at the crux of the problem with inspiration: *You can't depend on it.* The angelic choirs that fill your heart with brilliant and overflowing verbiage often won't be there when you need them. You're going to need a much more reliable and prosaic source of "song" to get you off your butt, to get you to stop procrastinating and get going. This point is so important that I shall assign it the honor of our fourth Swing Thought:

SWING THOUGHT NO. 4—*MATURE WRITERS DON'T WAIT FOR INSPIRATION. THEY DECIDE TO WRITE.*

—Inspiration is fine but undependable.
—It won't be there when you need it.
—Therefore, a serious writer *decides* to write as a choice.

Assignments that come with a deadline in effect insist that the writer produce irrespective of feeling. If you create assignments for yourself, always place deadlines on them. Deadlines don't phase the deliberate writer. The mature writer—the writer who is serious—won't need inspiration or freeze if they don't "feel" like writing. For example, the scariest part of book writing for me comes when a publisher sends a contract — a legally binding agreement wherein I guarantee to be creative enough to write an acceptable book by a specified date. An actionable promise to be creative, even artistic, within a looming time frame? Who's stupid enough to guarantee that? A deliberate, confident writer, that's who. I take a deep breath, sign the document, and then relax knowing I'm not a prisoner to the Nine Muses and Apollo. I have a method that never fails.

Deadlines test your skills at time management. The easiest way to get someone to put off a task is to give them more time. When you become a deliberate writer, you learn one of the secrets to greater productivity, namely, using the entire time allowed to your best advantage. When we get into the specifics of the writing process in Chapter Three, you'll see how to find your style, discover your voice, and make your content "real" and "relatable"—content in which you believe and have confidence.

In Review

Here are the two Swing Thoughts from Chapter Two.

3. The best way to learn a skill is to practice it. That holds true with writing.
4. Mature writers don't wait for inspiration. They *decide* to write.

Writing Prompts

Respond to the following.

1. From your everyday life, come up with at least five writing topics.
2. Pick one of those topics and write about it.
3. Do you procrastinate when it comes to writing? Why? Work it out on the page.

Reading Suggestions

1. "Once More to the Lake" by E.B. White—In this classic essay, White takes his son to the Maine lake that his dad took him to when he, White, was a kid. Then and there, White discovers a sobering truth about mortality and the toll of time on mortal humans. White's descriptions of the place "put you there."
2. "One Last Time" by Gary Soto—The author writes about his coming of age, working in the fields as a laborer and coming to terms with his Mexican heritage. Soto's essay provides a lesson in how a writer can make emotional states tangible.

3. "Hoppers" by Garrison Keillor—With his usual dry wit, Keillor makes an utterly ordinary event of puddle jumping into a revealing look at human quirks. Exhibit A in finding great topics in the most ordinary circumstances.

CHAPTER THREE

There Is No Such Thing as Writing

The title of this chapter might seem to be the most ridiculous thing a "how to" book on writing can declare. Your immediate instinct is to say, "Of course there is. I write. What do you mean, 'There's no such thing as writing?'"

What do I mean by that seemingly preposterous statement? Just this. What we call writing is the outcome of a process, what's produced only after following a series of steps in a sequential order. The outcome stems from steps that, like any other "recipe," must be followed to produce the desired result. Fortunately, unlike most recipes, *the writing process* contains lots of leeway allowing for individual expression and variation according to a person's particular needs and creativity. The important point for the developing writer is to understand the process and then adapt it to suit their individual style, needs, and circumstances. Harkening back to something we said in Chapter One, this is how one set of guidelines can be unique to writers of varying levels of ability.

The writing process should look familiar to you. Traditionally, it is presented in three steps:

1. Prewriting
2. Writing
3. Revision.

That's okay as far as it goes and it works fine as theory. However, anyone familiar with serious writing—for example, professional writers or those who write extensively for the workplace—know that the three-step sequence should actually be a five-step deal.

Here's the complete writing process, with the two additional steps italicized:

1. *Noise*
2. Prewriting
3. First draft
4. *Rest*
5. Revision.

As for the two additional steps, Step 1 has you scratching your head. Step 4 looks familiar but might seem puzzling, especially given your experiences with rushing to meet deadlines.

Over this chapter and the next, we'll address each of these five steps. As we do, try to plug in what I say into your specific situation.

Step 1: Noise and the Blank Page

You have one goal as a writer: To produce the best prose in the clearest and most efficient manner so you can communicate your ideas effectively to a reader or readers. Before you can do that, however, you need to clear the deck and eliminate the "noise." For our purposes, I define "noise" as any interference or obstacle, not just aural, that keeps you from doing optimum work. You'd be surprised how much noise there can be and usually is. You'd be equally shaken by how much of it you don't notice because of desensitization.

To do it well, writing demands large chunks of time and rooms of head space. Given the busy, hurried, and worrisome lives most people lead, you need to get both—that is, time and head space—in the best condition before you begin. Books on "how to write" and comp classes almost never mention noise, or, if they do, the tendency is to gloss over it. It's astounding how many would-be scribes skip this first step. They think they can just stop whatever they're doing and write. Addressing noise involves creating a kind of "safe room" meant only for writing as opposed to trying to squeeze in the work here and there, treating it as the lesser or least priority among your laundry list of responsibilities. *Real* writing requires a careful and deliberate look at your environment and temperament before you begin. You must place yourself in the best writing position that any particular situation will allow. Dribs and drabs won't do for accumulating the necessary time. Places antithetical to your creativity won't suffice as the location.

Writing requires intense focus. You best get that by purposely carving out of your busy schedule both the time and place to write. You will need to make time for it, just as you would for any other appointment or responsibility. To the extent you can control the clock, it won't be just *any* time but time best suited to your particular needs and circumstances.

In effect, when you've taken on the task of writing on deadline, somehow you have to find a way to dedicate significant blocks of time, energy, and effort to just you and the keyboard. Nothing less will do. Given all the other demands on you—social and personal, at work and home—that won't be easy, and don't expect it to be. Nonetheless, that doesn't faze the serious writer. It only scares away the dilettantes and dabblers.

Take a Look Around

You need to examine all the factors affecting your life and try to determine what conditions will work best. Once you figure that out, you should work to set up those conditions. Believe it: Writing under those "best conditions" will have a surprisingly good effect on your work. When and where you feel most comfortable? Figure it out. Are you a morning person or a night hawk? Do you prefer to write alone or with people around? Do you like music playing or must you have pin-drop silence? Such questions address noise.

A crying baby can be noise, literally. A personal problem? Noisy. The temptation to ditch your writing session for a night out with your pleading, partying friends? That, too, creates a cacophonous hurdle. Work pressures, household chores, dropping the kids off at the soccer game and picking them up, or even illness—these are just a few of the countless inconveniences of daily life that can, and will, affect your writing if you don't try to manage them. You can't eliminate all the distractions, obviously, but you can always skirt and quell some, maybe even most. Think "minimize," not "conquer," to be realistic about controlling the distractions and your writing target for the day.

Produce a plan that will put you in the best place and head space to write, then schedule it. Pencil it in as you would with any other important appointment. Try and incorporate some flexibility in case the unexpected should intrude, as it often does. Your plan will vary for each assignment and will likely change daily, sometimes several times a day, as life throws unforeseen challenges your way. This "looksee" examination doesn't take much time and can be as informal as making toast. If you skip this step, however, you'll find yourself trying to write on the fly, except that you'll never get off the ground. Writing has a kind of sentience about it. If you don't give it its proper due, it will "know" and that lack of respect will come back to haunt you where it hurts the most, on the page. In the same way, give it proper planning and your "inner writer" will be pleased, setting you up for your best work.

Here are some tips on how to create the best writing environment for yourself:

— **Balance.** What commitments do you have to other classes; to work; spouses, boyfriends, girlfriends, chums, family, and loved ones; sports, hobbies, and play time; personal needs? You need to strike a balance without shirking the writing, which must assume priority.

— **Time.** Amid all that, figuring out the best 15 minutes to get the entire project done won't cut it. Writing doesn't work in that one-and-done way, and it can't ever be an afterthought. Like walking for good health, writing is a cumulative activity. If you walk 3 times a day for 20 minutes, it's the same as getting in an hour's stroll. Same with writing: An hour here, two hours there, then three hours later gives you six hours of dedicated time.

— **Schedule.** Produce a writing schedule for the day or week and stick to it as best you can. Be flexible but also serious. If something upsets the schedule, don't get scrupulous or feel guilty. Simply adjust the schedule. If after you've done everything you can to free up time and you find none, you have two options: (a) Drop one of your other commitments or (b) admit that you won't be able to write. If you're serious about your work, you will have no qualms about making the tough choices. If you can't select (a) or (b), then forget it. You're not ready to write.

— **Environment.** If you had unlimited resources, what would your perfect writing space look like? You likely won't be able to fly to an island resort and compose by poolside sipping your favorite drink, but you might be able to approximate the conditions. Maybe it's downing Bud in the bathtub instead of savoring Johnny Walker Blue under the palms. I had one student who imagined writing in a fancy treehouse. She ended up making a corner of her room look like one.

Many writers like to be among others to compose. To accommodate that, coffee houses can do the trick. Do you need total silence and near-monastic serenity? Create it. Music? Slip on your headphones. Hip hop or classical? Your choice. Are you more comfortable writing first drafts on a yellow legal pad or spiral-bound notebook? Pen or pencil? Do you prefer doing first drafts on your computer? Longhand on paper? When I write, I will sometimes have another window on my computer screen showing a cheesy film with no sound. I'll often select a cheap Sci-Fi flick (*It Conquered the*

World) or a black-and-white horror film from the 1950s (*House on Haunted Hill*). Other times it's a silent comedy (Charlie Chaplin) or if I need to hear something, classical music. At other times, I must have silence and no distractions. Selecting which of these options depends on my mood that day. Perhaps it's like that with you. If so, do whatever it takes. These are important considerations, and it's a mistake to ignore them.

— **Have a Plan.** You can't produce your best work by randomly and haphazardly taking bits of time or, worse, waiting to the last possible moment and madly banging out something to technically fulfill the requirements of the assignment and meet your deadline. Yes, it satisfies the minimum requirements, but such force-fits usually fail. Planning addresses this critical issue. Find the time. You have a deadline to meet. This conveniently leads us into our next Swing Thought.

SWING THOUGHT NO. 5—*DEADLINES ARE SACRED.* A SERIOUS WRITER *NEVER* MISSES A DEADLINE.

— Treat all deadlines seriously.
— Carve enough time and find a good place to give the writing priority.
— If you miss a deadline, be honest. Don't make excuses, and never let it happen again.

Granted, sometimes life gets in the way, and it can't be helped. I recall an instance where a student missed her deadline because her house burned down. Another suffered a serious spill on the ice requiring hospitalization and many missed assignments. I remember a man having a heart attack during a seminar. I'm not saying your emergency has to be that drastic. Maybe you just had one of those weeks from hell or the worst bad-hair day of your life. The point is, if you have a legitimate reason for not fulfilling the requirements of an assignment or missing the deadline, your instructor, manager, or editor will usually be understanding and work with you, especially if all your other work has been competently done and diligently respectful of due dates. A good track record can ameliorate many a fluke situation. Be up front. There's usually a little time built into deadlines, though don't count on that safety net. Never give lame excuses of the "dog ate my homework" type. And don't make it a habit. Routinely counting on deadline extensions for no good reason springs a red flag of mistrust.

These are just a few examples of questions you need to look at before you write. It doesn't take too much time, and once you begin to pay attention to these "insignificant" factors, you will see that they're not so inconsequential. By becoming more aware of these things, you become more conscious of the conditions needed to write well, and greater awareness is priceless.

Step 2: Prewriting

After you have analyzed the favorable conditions and fit them into your schedule and lifestyle, you need to immediately make sure that you understand the assignment. If you create assignments for yourself, this will not be a problem. If you're doing that, it's best to be specific about what you're asking yourself to do. Always include a word count and a deadline. Then date and keep all work. Throw nothing away. This will give you a chain of evidence for review and a chart for progress.

Understanding what's being asked of you is a consideration so important we shall elevate it to Swing Thought status.

SWING THOUGHT NO. 6—CAREFULLY REVIEW EVERY ASSIGNMENT. MAKE SURE YOU UNDERSTAND WHAT'S REQUIRED.

— Never make assumptions or guess.
— If you have questions, always ask. Clarify as much as you need.
— If you have thoughts or feedback, be sure to share.

I can't tell you how many times I've had students hand in work and have it be a response to the wrong question or other such error (incorrect length, improper format, single-spaced, ink too light, distracting type face, too small or large type size). These errors show that the writer wasn't paying attention or guessing instead of clarifying. That produces a kind of feedback you don't want. If you're writing to complete an editorial assignment, there's almost no legitimate excuse for a writer to turn in something grossly out of sync with what their editor was expecting.

A publisher/editor of a lifestyle magazine once contracted me to write a monthly column about philosophy and spirituality. When I handed in my inaugural effort, the editor rejected it. He demanded a rewrite so extensive that nothing of what I originally wrote could be salvaged. When I looked back to reverse-engineer what went wrong, I found that we had both erred. The editor had failed to communicate clearly his wants. I had failed to pepper him with enough questions to pin him down regarding his needs, including what I saw was the odd subject matter for that publication. After a long phone call the next day, I resigned the gig. I didn't need the aggravation irrespective of the money, and the editor didn't need a writer who couldn't agree with his vision of the topic.

It's easy to assume that you know the assignment, but do you? Did you take the information down correctly? This takes on added importance if the assignment comes verbally and not in writing, as it did with my aborted lifestyle column. Are you clear about the topic? You need to make sure of this before you can get started. While it's okay to ask a fellow student or a sympathetic spouse, the best place to go for clarification is the instructor, editor, or supervisor. Go straight to the source.

Those Little Gears

Okay, you're clear on what you have to do. What's next? You might be surprised to hear this, but you've already begun. As soon as your brain takes in the directions of the assignment, you immediately and subconsciously begin to work. Yes, you're already prewriting, though probably you don't know it. That's what happens when you ask someone to perform any creative act. Those little gears on the right side of your brain begin turning. Put a piece of paper and some finger paints before a child and ask them to create a picture. They dive in, usually without hesitation. You will see on their faces the wheels at work. If you've ever looked at any artist pondering over a canvass, look at the face. It's there. I've even seen it in scientists and mathematicians working on problems. I've seen it in gardeners, quilters, and mountain climbers trying to plot a route. Sometimes a creative person becomes so engaged they'll stick out the tongue or squint their eyes. Their focus shoots lasers. Your mind works that way, too. It is predisposed to begin, so take advantage. Don't fight it. Go with the creative flow and encourage it. As best you can, become more aware of your thinking at this early stage.

Say you are asked to write about an experience that changed your life. Without consciously thinking, the gears begin to drive the cogs which power the pistons that produce the sparks to ignite the word fire. It happens instantly and repetitively, which suggests the importance of prewriting, that discipline that allows your thoughts, conscious and otherwise, to emerge.

*Prewriting refers to **everything** a writer does before they are ready to attempt a first draft.*

This includes many different activities, depending on the assignment. Obviously, writing from personal experience differs from writing about an unfamiliar topic.

For the first, you pretty much have the material stored in your head. You will do an inventory of memory. This involves a content analysis of your recollections. For the second, you'll do research.

Prewriting can include brainstorming, notetaking, free writing, fact-finding, memory scans, literature searches, arriving at a controlling idea (CI), and asking such questions as:

— What's my topic?
— Do I understand it?
— How much do I know about it?
— What kind of research will I have to do?
— Where will I find my material?
— What major point am I trying to make?
— What will be my attitude or tone with respect to readers? Do I want to make them happy? Sad? Angry? Do I want to rouse them into action? Am I trying to convince someone that my point of view on the topic is the correct one? Am I simply trying to share information in a neutral, objective fashion?
— What are the best methods to tell this story? Narrative? Comparison and contrast? Cause and effect? Argumentation? Classification and division? Some other technique? A combination? Later in the book, we'll examine these different rhetorical strategies.
— How am I going to organize the material?

The "Dirty Word" of Writing

That last question leads to a point that often causes heartburn in many writers. I'm speaking of an outline. To many, "outline" is the "dirty word" of writing, composition's F-bomb. Many developing writers skip this part of the writing process—or think they do. They actually don't.

They can't.

It's impossible not to outline. When I ask a room of writers, "How many of you do not outline before you begin writing?," a bunch of hands invariably raise, to which I would say, "Nonsense. That's not true." I've long suspected that some put up their hands as a show of bravado, as if to say "I'm so talented I don't need to plan." To me, they're whistling past the linguistic graveyard.

I would explain that everyone *has* to outline in some fashion before writing. Your brain gives you no choice. The only question is how effective they are in performing this task. Outlining incorporates not just formulating a writing plan but *any* work done from the moment you receive an assignment to the point where you're ready to begin the first draft. When I mentioned how the right side of your brain begins to activate the moment you are asked to perform any creative task, I'm referring to the subconscious activity that seeds your outline. It affects how you will ultimately cast your ideas. You only become aware of this when you allow this process expression and begin the organizing itself. That's when the left brain begins to examine the task and the material. When you properly outline, the ideas are like water contained under pressure looking for a crack through which to escape. The brain's left side then searches for shapes, order, connections, and logical links among the ideas.

The moment you receive an assignment, you go to work on it. Even if you do nothing more than read the assignment, you're thinking about it. Certainly, if you do nothing else before your first draft, you're putting one foot on a banana peel and the other at the edge of a cliff. Not much good can happen. You're still at the beginning stages of planning your approach. It's like you're the pilot and your subject is the airplane. You must plan your flight, file that plan, take off, stay on course, and land safely.

Realize then that you *do* outline. The question isn't about that. It's "Are you doing it effectively?"

Okay, you receive an assignment. So far so good. Despite what you may think, you're nowhere near being ready to write much less *write it real*. For our purposes here, when I say "write," I have a specific use in mind. "Write" refers only to a first draft and a first draft only. Any work before that is **prewriting**. Anything after is revision. That may be an alien concept, but grasping it produces one of the keys of effective prose.

Harken back to something I said earlier, that there's "no such thing as writing." The end product of what you see in the finished piece, the one you hand in and submit or some published piece that you read, isn't "writing." It's the product of **rewriting**. Every book you've ever read and every published piece in a newspaper, magazine, or online from a reputable source got there only through multiple rewrites.

To repeat: There's no such thing as writing, unless you refer to a first draft. There's only rewriting.

The next step is to come up with a plan. I hesitate to use the word "outline." When I was a student, "outline" was an expletive, an alphanumeric death march that stifled creativity and enthusiasm. I'm referring to the dreaded formal outline. You know what it looks like. Something like this:

I ————————————————————— -
  A. ————————————— -
  B. ————————————— -
  C. ————————————— -

    1. _____
    2. _____

      a. ————————————— -
      b. ————————————— -
      c. ————————————— -

        I ————————————
        ii _____
        iii _____
        iv _____

II ————————————————————— -
  A. ————————————————— -
  B. ————————————————— -

… and so on, until your head spins and you begin howling at the moon.

I call this the "straightjacket outline." The "Tower of Babel" would fit just as well. That's how my first college writing instructor (a nod to the late, great Mary Lawrence) referred to the formal outline. She called it a straightjacket for the way it forced rigidness, inflexibility, and mechanical formalism. Such an outline tends to bind a writer, turning creativity into captivity. An informal outline, though, which often is simply a few topics written down in some kind of strategic order, has a liberating effect.

I mentioned before that a writing plan resembles a set of blueprints. In each case, you're trying to develop a plan that will allow you to build a structure that holds together with no cracks in the basement, no leaks in the roof, and a floor plan that flows gracefully. You want what you build to withstand the outside elements and, within, provide a comfortable and satisfying space.

The straightjacket outline too often results in overkill, like using a shotgun instead of a swatter to kill a fly. Rather than giving the writer a set of plans that will build the house, the busyness of the traditional outline tends to produce plans for an overdesigned structure doomed to failure and collapse.

What usually happens when an instructor requires you to hand in a straightjacket outline? You write your essay first, and *then* you create a detailed outline that matches it exactly, like a set of perfectly matched salt and pepper shakers. Confess. You've probably done this. I know I did, before Ms. Lawrence taught me otherwise.

Using a formal outline for most writing is fake. That's not how real writing works.

For longer pieces such as a senior thesis, a 20,000-word article, or a book, some version of this type of formal outline might be helpful (I say "might"), but for most of your writing—certainly with word counts under 5,000 words—a formal outline too often has counterintuitive effects.

Let me share a little "inside baseball" about this book. When I first got the idea, I went mentally through the classes and workshops I've taught on writing plus the questions people would ask at lectures and readings. I then considered my professional output of essays; news articles; editorials and think pieces; columns; scripts for movies, radio, and TV; books; plays; advertising copy; plus the editing of several books and countless other pieces. What did I do to make these assignments succeed? What insights did I share with my classes and at seminars and workshops? On a yellow legal pad, I jotted my ideas down as they occurred to me. I organized them into a semblance of order that would become the chapters of this book. That was it for my outline. The end result you hold in your hand, about 60,000 words that convey the distillation of that experience.

The major problem with the straightjacket outline is that it assumes something preposterous. It assumes that the writer has a minutely detailed knowledge of what will come out on paper or screen *before the writing actually begins*. That's nonsense, an absurdity worthy of Samuel Beckett. How can you possibly know the details of what you will produce until you actually produce it? In art, a painter such as Norman Rockwell worked from photos (his "outline") to reproduce the image in realistic detail. He knew beforehand what the painting would look like. In writing, it can't be done. To continue with the art analogy, the writer is like Jackson Pollock armed with paints and a blank canvass. He has a rough idea of what to do but doesn't know where the work will go until it has gone. Many an abstract painter, sculptor, and musician has created first and then "explained" after. It's the "I meant to do that" approach Writers of nonfiction prose aren't allowed such "wisdom," which almost always is seen in hindsight's rear-view mirror.

When you have a workable plan, and only then, are you *ready to write*.

In Review

Swing Thoughts from Chapter Three

5. Make sure you fully understand assignments.
6. Serious writers never miss a deadline.

Writing Prompts

The following prompts are for self-diagnostics. Be honest and detailed in your responses. Writing about these situations can help you pinpoint trouble areas.

1. What situations account for the "noise" that get in the way of your writing?
2. How have you typically handled the prewriting phase?
3. What's your experience with outlining? Troubleshoot the way you outline and do some reverse engineering.

Suggestion for Reading

1. Harvard College Writing Center, writingcenter.fas.harvard.edu—This site has an informative discussion. The irony is that after describing how to outline, it includes a sample "straight-jacket" formal outline.
2. "How to Write an Essay Outline" by Jack Caulfield—The author offers his take on essay mapping.
3. "Outlining" eapfoundation.com—Pragmatic presentation on brainstorming ideas, features of a good outline, and a checklist. Discusses key factors such as parallelism, coordination, and subordination.

CHAPTER FOUR

Write for the Reader, Not Yourself

In the previous chapter, we discussed outlining. Now I will let you in on a little secret: No matter how well you outline a piece, once you begin writing your first draft, you will find your topic revealing things you hadn't anticipated and could not have anticipated. The outline provides the launch mechanism for the writing to take off into the atmosphere of its full intention. This happens because your conscious mind taps into your unconscious storehouse. It finds overlooked but relevant material. That new material forces its way into sight. It wants to be seen and heard. When you look and listen, your writing leaves the runway and begins to fly.

The effect can be explosive. You might (and probably will) discover amazing new insights into the topic. Most every writer has enjoyed that grand experience when they come up with something good, even great. After they read what they wrote, they ask "How did I know that?" It's a wonderful feeling when you nail it. You'll hear it, too, when a writer says something like, "I didn't know what I thought until I read what I wrote."

On the other hand, sometimes you will write about topics that elicit raw memories and stinging emotions you're not ready to handle. This can happen especially when the words delve into emotionally traumatic experiences. Yes, such areas can be addressed productively, effectively, and even therapeutically, but you have to be ready. You'll know when the time comes. I had a student in a senior-level writing course who responded to an assignment about a life-changing incident.

She wrote about how her "stage mother" ruined her skating career and joy the sport gave her. She couldn't finish the piece, which bore the great title of "Dust on the Blades." The memory of her mother's pressure to win competitions at all cost was still too barbed for her to deal with in writing. The young woman confessed that she hadn't skated for several years. This is a great example of the sheer power of words. Or think about how long it took to write candidly and truthfully about the Vietnam conflict. It took more than a decade of processing and healing from the wounds. Only then could the books and films be created and released. The words will tell you if you are ready to address the topic at hand. Pay careful attention to your emotions.

The first draft will produce twists and turns within and among the paragraphs that surprise, a good sign of writing coming to life. Outlining in too much detail tends to stifle such surprises.

As we've seen, a fully formed outline before the first draft is absurd. Don't do it. Let the material determine the ultimate direction in draft copy. The outline must always yield to the creative impulse of the actual writing. It should be present but not visible, much like a skeleton. Every good piece of writing gives evidence of its outline, but this supporting structure lies just under the skin, unseen. A good outline is like the map you consult before a trip. GPS will indicate what it thinks is the best route, but when you get on the actual road, you'll often find detours, construction, gridlock, shortcuts, and other variations from the pre-plotted plan, illustrating that clean-room algorithms must occasionally bow to down-and-dirty reality.

Let Your Writing "Breathe"

To *write it real*, you need to let the writing "breath" as you compose. Once you have roughed out your plan, allow your words to take flight. Don't misunderstand, however, and here we must emphasize that while you probably don't need the straightjacket outline, you do need a plan. Without a plan, you'll wander aimlessly in a prose desert without enough water supplied by the right words assuming the correct order.

So what do you do? We reveal all in Swing Thought No. 7.

SWING THOUGHT NO. 7: AN OUTLINE IS A PRELIMINARY OR *PROVISIONAL GRASP* OF YOUR MATERIAL, SUBJECT TO CHANGE.

— Writing without a plan produces aimless work.
— Forget the formal outline. A few main thoughts in a coherent sequence will suffice.
— Let the outline serve the writing and not the other way around.

A working outline delineates your *best guess* at how to present material to the reader. Only this, and nothing more (with a nod to Eddy Poe).

This raises another significant point. Few things will scare a reader more than the feeling that they're reading something disorganized, "going nowhere," has no master plan or method, and not moving in a coherent and logical direction. As soon as your reader has a sense of "wandering," they jump out of the nosediving craft and pull the ripcord. The captain may go down with the ship and you may sink with your writing, but readers? Nothing doing. They book.

The time and effort put in (or not) during prewriting will show up in the finished work. Spend the sweat equity, and your writing will reflect that effort. Skip this phase and begin to write before you're ready, and your words will look like someone put them in a Vitamix blender and spilled them randomly onto the page. The reader should never be asked to fit together the pieces of a written work as if they were putting together a jigsaw puzzle. That's the writer's job.

Writing doesn't "just happen." It's a deliberate act, like any other specialized and difficult skill. You have to work on it. There's a great story involving the piano virtuoso Vladimir Horowitz. He had just performed a concert during which the audience demanded four curtain calls. After the performance at a "meet-and-greet" for high-ticket donors, a woman came up to the elderly Horowitz and said, "Oh, maestro! I'd give my life to play as beautifully as you." Without missing a beat, Horowitz replied, "Madam, that's exactly what I have done."

Do you want to be a virtuoso or just "good enough" to get by? Mastery or mediocrity? How far do you want to go with your writing? There's actually no ceiling, only the limitations found at the intersection of time, talent, effort, and determination.

Are you doing the heavy lifting when it comes to planning? If not, you can't possibly produce your best work or even "a reasonable facsimile thereof."

It might help to put this into perspective. You're doing all this work prior to actually putting words on a page not for yourself but for the reader. Time for our next Swing Thought.

SWING THOUGHT NO. 8: *WRITE FOR THE READER.*

— Your goal is to communicate. You can only do that as a creative act of extension, your ideas conveyed to that most valuable person, the reader.
— The reader completes the process of writing. If no one reads your work, you might as well keep a locked diary or not simply bother to write.
— As best you can, consider your likely audience. Different readers will have different needs.

Unless you're keeping a private journal or diary, you write so you can be read. That reader almost always has no emotional connection to you. Maybe it's your instructor or perhaps the thousands of readers of a newspaper or a blog. Perhaps it's management at your workplace. Your best friend or parents might look at your writing and gush with high praise, but they would do so even if the writing was terrible. They love you. They don't want to hurt your feelings.

Most readers don't have such built-in bias, and, as a writer, don't count on it. Your writing will live or die based on its quality, simple as that. An editor will spare no barbs if you hand in junk. You'll have one slip to learn the hard way—or go back to asking "Do you want butter on your popcorn, ma'am?" Writers must develop a thick skin, that "hard bark" I mentioned in the Foreword. Feedback's going to come fast and furious, so toughen up. It's not personal.

Think of readers as impartial consumers of your words. Each word, after all, is a conceptual tool with which you build writing that reflects the depth, intricacy, and quality of your thinking. The reader only has your words. You won't be there to explain what you meant or annotate any hidden meanings. They will likely know little about you personally. They will have none of the support systems that led to the words you chose. They won't be hip to your planning or rationale. They won't care about the difficulties you had to overcome. The words and words alone must do all the talking.

Vocabulary and Volumes

This leads to a brief word about vocabulary and syntax. You can't ever have enough words. Be hungry. Devour new words. When you come across a new word, look it up. Commit it to memory. Start to use it. During the first glimmerings that I might want to become a writer, I assigned myself daily vocabulary exercises. Each day I promised to learn at least one new word. By year's end, I would be assured of expanding my vocabulary by at least 365 words. It usually came to about double that amount. There are many ways to do this. You're smart. Figure out what works for you, then begin.

Vocabulary encompasses the words. Syntax decides the order of those words. Unlike painting, sculpture, or most music, writing conveys meaning linearly, one word at a time. Those other forms of art produce meaning through nonverbal, near-instantaneous effects. In writing, one word follows the next then the next and so on. That's how a writer produces it. That's how a reader reads it. The words combine into phrases, sentences, and paragraphs. One instant way to improve your writing is to learn new words and increase your reading, what I call the "Vocab and Volumes" approach. The first provides more options for expression, while the second allows you to "hear" what good writing, especially syntax, sounds like.

Consider this example:

The Red Sox won decisively.

Now change the syntax and tweak the vocabulary:

The Red Sox steamrolled to a decisive victory.
In convincing fashion, the Red Sox secured the win.

Each sentence conveys the same basic thought, but through vocabulary and syntax each assumes a slightly different meaning producing subtle but noticeable effects. English is an action language, with an estimated 50,000 verbs. Good writers take advantage of this by preferring the active voice.

"Voice" refers to what happens to a subject with respect to the verb in a given sentence. Does the subject perform the action (if so the verb is in active voice) or is it being acted upon (then the verb is in the passive voice)? Look at these examples:

Weak passive: Her singing was appreciated by the audience.
Strong active: The audience appreciated her singing.
Weak passive: Panetti was reassigned by the company.

Strong active: The company reassigned Panetti.
Weak passive: After a week of grueling practice, his greatest game was played by Jones.
Strong active: After a week of grueling practice, Jones played his greatest game.

Active voice projects energy and provides force and emphasis in writing, taking full advantage of the power of verbs. In fact, relying on the active voice is one of the easiest and most effective ways that writers can inject more "juice" their work, like giving their work an instant tune-up. The passive voice does have legitimate use, particularly when you want emphasis placed upon the subject, as in this sentence:

On April 14, 1865, President Lincoln was shot and killed by Booth.

Sometimes writers deliberately choose the passive voice when they want to hide the responsible parties, as in:

At the final session, the amendment was approved.

Notice how the passive voices hides the identities of the approvers.

With your proverbial neutral reader, you are attempting to achieve a supremely important and often difficult thing: You're trying to *communicate* your ideas to someone so that they get the full impact of what you're trying to tell them.

Allow me to share an elegant, effective example of word choice. In his poem "Those Winter Sundays," Robert Hayden writes about how his father would get up every day of the week "in the blueblack cold," build a fire to warm the house, and provide the oft-mundane, dreary actions of a loving parent, such as polishing his son's shoes for Sunday services. Hayden expresses guilt because he never thanked his father for those sacrifices.

In the poem's first line, Hayden writes: "Sundays too my father got up early …" The reader gets two words into the poem and already knows the father rose this way *every day of the week*. He didn't even get Sunday off. The word "too" tells us that. Omit "too," and the poem loses meaning and impact. A necessary concept explained by adding one word: That's writing of the highest magnitude.

Always ask: What will make the writing easier to understand? What can you do to make your meaning clearer and more interesting? This includes everything from syntax and word choice to paragraph order and physical layout.

Try to find out as much as you can about your reader(s). Is the audience general as in mass circulation media, or specialized, for example, trade associations or fraternal groups? Often, newspapers, magazines, and online publications will have detailed information on its readers—how many, ages, income, education, and more. Ask about those demographics. For instance, if you wrote an article on the dangers of scuba diving, the direction and tone will dramatically differ if the audience consists of the readers of a general-interest magazine or a group of diving instructors attending a workshop.

Readers *Do* Judge Books by the Cover

You've heard the expression "You can't judge a book by its cover."

Actually, you can and you do. The first thing someone does when they pick up a book for the first time is to look at the title, then the graphic presentation. Many times they'll peruse or put it down based upon appearance. Your typed manuscript produces a similar effect. There can only be one and only one first impression of your work. Produce neat, presentable manuscripts, whether online or hard copy. You would no more show up on a job interview with filthy clothes than you would turn in work that conveys lack of care. Hand in sloppy work, and you begin on the wrong foot.

Keep in mind mechanics and appearance. You want to spell correctly with good grammar and usage. Every time your readers find a typo or a grammatical flaw, such as subject–verb agreement, they lose confidence. They begin to doubt. As a writer, you want to be taken seriously. Carelessness won't do it.

Abbreviations and shortcuts when texting friends may work well for that purpose. Readers of texts aren't expecting finished prose, and you're not trying to produce *War and Peace* or even *Harry Potter and the Sorcerer's Stone*. You write hurriedly, usually in the fewest keystrokes possible, as in "I h8 txtng."

There's a great debate (gr8 db8) concerning texting's effects on language and communication, and we won't get into that here. First, we don't have the room. Second, that's not the purpose of this book. Suffice it to say that when you shift from informal to formal writing, you must be aware of the change and adjust your writing accordingly. You can't write "btw" for "by the way" or b4 for "before" in formal prose without being branded a lightweight.

As you probably know, there are different forms of our language other than Standard American English (SAE). As linguists agree and the volume of publishable prose confirms, SAE is a real and necessary commodity for anyone engaging in formal writing. This does not diminish the viability of other forms of communication such as texting or African American Vernacular English (AAVE). In fact, the opposite is true. Both texting and AAVE have valid, even irreplaceable uses, especially with peer readers as proven by the emergence of these types of English in response to obvious contextual need. They usually reflect speaking (the vernacular) and informal communication as opposed to the accepted conventions of formal writing.

As all matters in writing, what form of English one chooses boils down to choice. Most publishing outlets expect SAE, but the choice to use SAE to appeal to these expectations or to use non-SAE dialects instead is and should be left up to the writer. Using non-SAE dialects is a political choice and a personal preference. Like all choices, such decisions have positive and negative consequences that the writer should consider in making their decisions. Whichever form of English you choose, you must be prepared to accept the consequences of your choice. In writing, freedom is not license. Don't confuse the two.

America doesn't have language academies, although it has linguists and organizations such as the Modern Language Association, style books, and handbooks that establish standards—conventions—that set the accepted forms to be used in more formal communication.

As far as speaking is concerned, there isn't one standard of American English. Any visit to the Northeast, say Boston, then to the deep South will drive home the point. Speaking and writing, though, differ dramatically. Speakers have enormous leeway, as slang, jargon, and the vernacular illustrate. Speakers, especially in informal situations, are off the hook for repetition, oral "tics" such as "um" and "uh," imprecision, sloppiness, circularity, and other "mistakes." Speakers, other than those reading from a text, "compose" instantly in-the-moment and can't be expected to achieve high-level rhetorical muster (though it's good if they can). Writers of formal prose don't enjoy these breaks. Writers, though, have the luxury of time in which to take their words, work with them, and revise them. Readers therefore expect good grammar, correct spelling, strong diction (choice of words), linearity, few wasted words, and directness.

Using SAE is nothing more than showing linguistic good manners in response to the expectations of the majority of editorial requirements and publishing outlets. That's all it is. Ultimately, the accepted form of a language is a social construct. With clear communication as its end, especially in the production of written and verbal content, society determines what works best. Political or moral judgments shouldn't and usually don't decide this; they only go for what actually works most effectively for the greatest number of people in the greatest number of situations.

As for AAVE, also called Black English or Ebonics, sociolinguists consider it a "contact language," primarily a form of spoken English that achieves its highest use as a dialect. For speaking and writing, it's as valid as SAE (or any other form of social English for that matter). For entertainment and emotional expressions, it can elevate into an art form, as rap and hip-hop have musically demonstrated. For formal writing (your job, for example) or publishable work, though, writers, editors, and readers generally prefer SAE over the many other forms and varieties of English. The same holds true in writers for whom English is a second language.

In any case, if you choose a dialect other than standard SAE, it's best to communicate beforehand with your immediate receiver, be it an editor, publisher, manager, boss, or instructor.

You are best advised to make your work stand out and shine not just through content but also through appearance, adhering to the accepted conventions of standard English, including spelling and grammar. Ignoring conventions, directives, and guidelines can send the wrong message and can draw unwanted attention to appearance rather than content. It can even suggest you don't care. That may not be the case, but why risk stacking the odds against you? Writing is hard enough as it is. If it conveys the perception that you don't care enough to respect your own work, why should the reader? Neat, technically correct writing doesn't guarantee brilliance, but sloppy, ungrammatical, and inappropriate prose assures rejection.

Granted, poets and fiction writers often break the rules and veer off into strange linguistic lands that are usually off limits to prose. Poetry and fiction represent separate and distinct rhetorical categories in which convention can often be ignored and to great effect. Prose writers don't enjoy such leeway. Their travel visas limit them to areas on the map, so to speak.

Punctuation Makes the Reader's Job Easier

Submit your work in the form and format required. For instance, when preparing the final draft of this book, the publisher sent me its in-house style sheet. As best I could, I tried to make the manuscript conform to those requirements. I didn't ask why. The publisher decided the preferable format, saving me the hassle.

If the assignment calls for double-spacing the text, page numbering at lower left, with 12-point Times New Roman typeface, present it that way. If you can choose your own format, make it neat, clean, and legible. If not, always follows the directives issued with the assignment. Avoid fancy typefaces such as script or anything that's hard to read. Simple and clean works best.

Or take proper punctuation. Please (apologies to comic Henny Youngman, for whom I once wrote jokes).

Punctuation makes reading easier by conveying the "music" of the words. Pauses, slowdowns, stops, and starts play as much a part in conveying meaning as the other tools of writing.

When writing first developed, writers tended to string words together one after another without stops, breaks, or any other indication for pausing or slowing down. Writing flitted from idea to idea with no advance notice, delaying widespread literacy by decades and maybe centuries. For instance, try reading ancient documents prior to the arbitrarily selected date of 1500 A.D. in their original presentation. You brain will soon begin to smoke.

Unpunctuated writing dates back to the ancient Greeks, who wrote their manuscripts without spaces between individual letters, asinthissentence. In the 3rd century BCE, the Greek playwright Aristophanes began inserting tiny dots between thoughts to make scripts easier for actors to read aloud. When the Roman Empire surpassed Greece as the West's leading power, though, they dumped Aristophanes' refinement and wentbacktonospacing. That's how writing stood for another thousand years or so.

Use your search engine to examine a copy of the Magna Carta, the epic, rights-producing document signed by English King John at Runnymede in 1215. Then try to read those long, narrowly spaced lines, with tiny lettering and almost no punctuation. You'll soon be singing "They're Coming to Take Me Away, Ha-Haa!" by Napoleon XIV, a hit novelty tune from 1966. Yeah, you'll go that far gone.

What we now understand as punctuation began developing with the Christian monks around the year 800 or thereabout. Their task was to copy ancient manuscripts, and, in doing so, they saved Western Civilization. The copyists began to devise individual systems of punctuation. When the French King Charlemagne caught wind of this practice, he ordered a monk named Alcuin to take these individual systems and develop a standardized series of marks that today we recognize as punctuation. It took centuries before punctuation became the convention of Western writing, but the work had begun. As they say, the mills of the gods grind s-l-o-w-l-y, but they grind exceedingly well.

Fortunately, because of the grammatical guidelines that have been developed over the centuries, today's readers don't have an eye-straining and brain-numbing ordeal. That's why you must be diligent about following proper conventions with respect to grammar, spelling, and punctuation. It's not for you. It's for the reader. Reading can be a chore. Give readers any excuse to give up on you, and they will.

The Controlling Idea (CI): Writing's "North Star"

Back to outlines. What should yours look like? It can be as simple as a few jottings on a sticky note. It can look like a bicycle wheel, the so-called "spoke outline" where you place your controlling idea in the middle with supporting ideas shooting out as "spokes." There's no one way it has to look. The important thing is to get your ideas on paper in a way that works best for you when you begin the task of hammering out a first draft.

By the time you've finished brainstorming and come up with the supporting details, you should have a clear idea of what you want to say. We're talking about the *theme* of your piece, the overall point. Even a one-paragraph assignment will have a theme unless it's pure description. For instance, it's one thing to simply describe a baseball: A white sphere with yarn and string wound around a hard rubber center and covered with two pieces of horsehide held together by 108 red stitches, 9 inches in circumference, 3 inches in diameter, weighing 5 ounces. The stark description goes nowhere. If, however, you write an essay about the baseball's production, you might have a theme centered on exploited foreign workers at the factory that manufactures the balls.

I prefer the term *controlling idea* (CI) to theme because it tells you exactly what it is. "Theme" sounds vague and cottony. "Controlling Idea" has a more substantial, precise conveyance. It tells you what it means.

A CI steers the direction of the entire piece, the overall point you wish to make. If someone asks, "Hey, what's your essay about?" they're asking for your CI. You should be able to state it in a *complete sentence*, not a phrase or a fragment.

Here are a few quick examples of a CI:

CI: *When I became a nurse, I learned about true compassion.*
Not: *Learning compassion.*
CI: *The stock market crashed because of emotion not logic.*
Not: *The stock market crash.*
CI: *The Patriots won because of a superb game plan.*
Not: *Game planning.*

A well-formed CI helps you realize your overarching purpose. It acts like the North Star does in celestial navigation. Pioneers, wagon trains, hikers, and other outdoor adventurers have long used the North Star for direction. The North Star, seen in the night skies of the Northern Hemisphere, lies in a direct line from the two stars that form the right side of the "Big Dipper" (*Ursa Major*). Though the Dipper rotates during the four seasons, the two stars on the far side of the cup will always point to the North Star. Once you locate that star, you will know true north and from there, south, east, and west.

Do I Leave It in or Cut It?

One of the most important and difficult decisions a writer faces will be what material to include and what to discard. Having a strong CI helps immensely. Material that doesn't contribute to your overall point should be cut. Include only the material that advances the writing.

Your CI will help you spot this extraneous material. By asking yourself "Does this passage advance the overall point?" you have a measure against which you can place the material in question. If it's relevant, keep it. If it wanders, discard it or find another place where it better fits, and be ruthless about the choice.

In Review

Here are the Swing Thoughts from Chapter Four:

> 7. An outline is a *preliminary* grasp of your material.
> 8. Write for the reader. Do anything that will help the reader.

Writing Prompts

1. Develop an outline for an essay on the subject of your choosing.
2. In the outline from Question 1, what is your CI? Write it in the form of a complete sentence.
3. Now write the essay based on your response to the first two questions.

Reading Suggestions

1. "Politics and the English Language" by George Orwell—One of the great essays in the English language. Orwell follows how bureaucracy and narrowmindedness have infected English, leading to its deterioration. He traces the causes of poisoned prose, lists his famous six rules of writing, and shares the prescription for a cure.
2. "Clutter" from William Zinsser's *On Writing Well*—Another classic. Zinsser's warm style suitably adapts to his purpose: A good writer writing about writing and teaching others to write well. He's a stickler in some respects but inevitably stresses the correct details.
3. "Those Winter Sundays" by Robert Hayden—One of my favorite poems of all time. Hayden looks back on the life of his deceased father and realizes how much his dad showed his love with daily care. He wishes he had thanked him for "making banked fires blaze" to warm up the cold house and for the countless other thankless jobs his dad performed. The poem exemplifies how brilliant economy of diction can convey profundity in few words. Yes, it's poetry, but the lessons still apply to prose.

CHAPTER FIVE

First Draft, Rest, and Revision

Step 3: First Draft

Okay. Now it's time to put words on paper or screen. "Finally," you might say, but the preparation you put in up to that point will pay off big time and separate you from all the others who refuse to do the hard work leading up to the first draft.

Most other writing texts, style books, and books on composition will call this step "writing." My book doesn't. Our third step is a first draft only.

A first draft is just that. The adjective "first" implies more to come—a second, third, fourth, and so on. It's not unusual for a writer to go through six, seven, eight—countless—revisions, even into double figures. The first draft has hewn the overall figure from the prepared stone of prewriting. Revision then keeps refining and chipping away here, adding there, adding focus, detail, nuance, coherence, and development until the work is finished.

Let me get at it another way.

When I use the word "writing," I'm referring to the finished piece. The sad truth is that too many developing writers believe that when you've done the first draft and maybe a quickie revision, you've done the writing. Not so, not by a long shot. They believe "first word = best word." That equation holds true for informal writing, but formal prose places much greater demands on you.

In his classic essay "Politics and the English Language," George Orwell makes three overall points. First, he says the English language is in decline. Second, he writes that with remedial action, the deterioration can be reversed. Third, he says that without the proper attention and care, the slide will continue until the language becomes second rate or, worse, a propagandistic device used to obscure truth, giving "the appearance of solidity to pure wind." One look at much of today's "disinformation" suggests we are in that third phase.

Orwell makes the point that effective prose "doesn't just happen." It is the product of difficult, exacting work. If you can't make friends with this fact, you will likely forever assign your writing to the bargain basement. Once there, you'll discover that such a cellar contains no bargains but much abasement.

A first draft represents your initial approach to the material. Once you begin that first attempt, you'll likely make good beginnings as well as false starts, getting some things right and some things wrong and that's okay, as our next Swing Thought states.

SWING THOUGHT NO. 9: *THERE'S NO SUCH THING AS A "BAD" FIRST DRAFT. REVISION SEES TO THAT.*

— The goal in your initial attempt should be to plow through the draft from beginning to end.
— A first draft supplies the comfort and assurance of subsequent cracks at the material.
— Having a first draft gives you something to which you can react.

"What," you say. "My drafts are terrible!"

No problem.

From Start to Finish

After that first draft you can, should, and will go back to it for improvement. What you get right, retain. What you get wrong, fix. Kurt Vonnegut said that revision allowed his otherwise jumbled work to achieve a semblance of clarity, the chance to approximate articulateness. He was joking but only to make a serious point.

By far the best writing strategy for a first draft is to complete your piece from beginning to ending. This won't happen every time, but with shorter pieces (under 2,000 words to pick a number), that should be your goal. This stresses the importance of what we said about being "ready to write." A writer is ready when the prewriting is done and there's a plan with a CI in hand. At that point, you've assembled the ingredients. You should then be able to produce a roughly completed work.

You won't always be able to go from start to finish, although with proper planning that usually can be done. Often writers stumble on openings. In Chapter Seven, we'll look at specific strategies on how to get going up front, how to develop the middle, and how to convincingly conclude.

If you can't go wall-to-wall, try to produce as much as you can, especially the body or middle of the essay, because that's where you'll develop the core of the material. Pausing in a first draft to find just the right word or phrase can cause brain freeze that stops you in your tracks. It doesn't have to be that way. For the sections giving you pause, do the best you can and try to write something, even if it's junk that serves as a placeholder.

Something to look for in writing the first draft: Is the writing taking a direction you didn't anticipate? Are you learning more about the material as you go along? Are you seeing new connections between and among the different ideas? Did any new discoveries emerge? Such developments indicate that the writing is coming to life. One thing's for sure. When the topic engages a prepared writer, pleasant surprises will occur. Often you will only begin to discover your most penetrating insights in the first draft. No amount of planning seems to unearth them, but once you get the words going, there they are. As someone once put it, "How do I know what I think until I see what I say?" It goes back to outlines, where you make educated guesses about the work. Once you get into the "deep muddy" of the first draft, the actual direction emerges.

The importance of starting early becomes apparent when your first draft goes awry, as will often happen. Sometimes you need to write what *doesn't* work to discover what does. False starts and dead ends reveal much, and, if handled properly, they can provide the writer with vital directional clues. Having begun the work early, the writer now has sufficient time to recover—a far different scenario than if you waited until the night before or "the morning of." You then have to hand in hurried writing that goes nowhere. The reader will spot it on the first page.

Step 4: Rest

Composition texts, style books, and handbooks almost never mention this important step. Neither do most instructors. When I was working on a daily newspaper as a budding journalist, I learned a big lesson about writing and editing. Mostly, I worked as an editor on the copy desk or telegraph desk. I would also contribute columns and other writing—arts and entertainment reviews, personality profiles, and other pieces.

The Syracuse Post-Standard was a large metropolitan daily with a vast circulation area and seven daily editions. The first edition, "the Bulldog," came first because the delivery trucks had to get it to circulation areas most distant from Syracuse, as far north as the Canadian border. I remember once coming back from the newsroom needing to write a review of a Queen/Thin Lizzy concert. I had about 30 minutes to meet the deadline for the Bulldog. City editor George Carr had given me a piece of advice. He said, "No matter how little time you have to hand in your story, take a break before you revise. Even if you have just 10 minutes before deadline, when you finish your draft, take a walk to the water fountain. Get a drink and walk back. In that short time," George said, "try to forget about the piece."

To effectively transition from draft to revision, you need to switch your brain. That's really what George was telling me. A first draft is a *creative* activity. You're producing writing that has never existed. Creation engages the right side of your brain. Revision *analyzes* something that already exists. Analysis is a left-side activity. If you try to revise a first draft too soon, especially while you're writing, you will experience a literal brainstorm. The left and right sides of your brain will be at war. Developing writers fare poorly under these conditions; a fuzzy murkiness freezes them in place. That's what's going on with so-called "writer's block." You're trying for perfection when the goal should be to get a preliminary draft from start to finish as best you can and as unpolished as it usually is.

"Writer's Block"

You'll notice I use the phrase "writer's block" in quotation marks. I use quotes because the so-called "writer's block" doesn't exist. It is always possible to write something. For instance, you can **free-write** and begin jotting down the first things that come into your head. Let's say the topic is gardening. Here's what free writing looks like:

> *Gardening's not for everyone. You need the "green thumb," or do you? Some people are "all thumbs" however to say nothing of Tom Thumb or thumbing a ride. Hitchhiking? Not cool. You never know who's going to pick you up. Unlucky with planting? My tomatoes come out looking like pineapples. Insects and pests. Beetle traps work and slugs will go to a happy death drinking beer. Don't wear good*

clothes unless you want them full of mud. Dig your hands into the soil. The dirt produces all life. Amazing, another of those daily miracles we overlook. Thou art dust and unto dust thou shalt return.

Gibberish, right? Well, most of it. Actually, I can see the seeds for at least three interesting essays.

You can **brainstorm**. You have your topic and think of anything about it that comes to mind. You blitz and list ideas without judgment or evaluation. The topic is space travel in the 1960s. Brainstorming might look like this.

— *Apollo moonshot.*
— *Limited computing power.*
— *Scientists are idealists.*
— *Math flew the mission on paper first.*
— *More computing power in your phone than moon mission.*
— *Gemini, Mercury, Apollo. Greek gods. Humanity's intruding on the heavens.*
— *Stanley Kubrick did not fake the moon landing.*
— *JFK speech.*
— *Get there first. Beat the Soviets.*
— *Cold War proxy.*
— *Heat and cold. Airless. Protection. Vulnerability.*
— *Houston, we have a problem.*
— *Navigation.*
— *Everyday products from space program. Freeze-dried food. Tang.*
— *Cost worth it?*
— *Robots vs. humans.*
— *Sci-fi movies.*

This can go on and on. Once more, there are seeds for several promising leads.

Another way to beat writer's block I call **Tape-'n-Type**. You speak about your topic into a recorder. Play it back and transcribe. Smart phones can transcribe *while* you talk. This gets you into handling words, just the warmup you often need to jumpstart actual writing.

Another method I call **Copy That**. *This technique never fails.* Take a piece of writing that you admire. Make sure it's written by someone else. The important thing is that you enjoy reading it. Begin copying the passage, word for word. Processing the words tricks your brain into mimicking the activity it directs when you write your own material. Pretty soon, you'll loosen up and begin to write.

Now back to Step 4 of the writing process—Rest. Pausing to "get away" from the writing helps you make the shift from creation (you're the artist) to analysis (you're the engineer). Only then can you revise (and revive) your work to greater effectiveness. Look at the word "revision." It begins with the prefix "*re*" from the Latin, which means "again" or "back." Thus, re-vision literally means to "see again" or "go back to it once more." Rest helps you see the writing with new eyes.

As best as you can, try to develop distance from what you've written. You need to be more clinical, less falling in love with your words. Pretend you're looking at someone else's writing. Be objective and clinical, not obtuse and cynical.

Consider making a writing schedule. If, for example, you have a week to complete the assignment, a division of time might look like this:

Day 1 and 2: Eliminate noise (Step 1) and Prewrite (Step 2).
Day 3: First draft (Step 3).
Day 4: Rest (Step 4).
Day 5 and 6: Revise (Step 5).
Day 7: Proof and submit.

Notice how you built in a full day of rest. Longer deadlines allow more time for that, shorter ones less. The important point is to not to start revising too quickly after your first draft or, worse, during the writing of your first draft. As you gain more experience with the writing process, you'll be able to produce better first drafts and also incorporate more editing as you go along. For now, try to keep first draft and revision separate to let the words settle.

Writing is not like math, where the process and the results are cut-and-dried; two plus two always equals four no matter how many times you add them up or how many different people do it. Any other answer except four will be incorrect. With writing, every time it will be different. You can have 30 people writing about the same topic, and you will end up with 30 different responses. The quality of those responses relies not just on objective criteria as in math but also the subjectivity of the individual writer and reader, for it is tricky to specify what separates great writing from good, good from average, and average from poor. As Supreme Court Justice Byron Potter said about pornography, it's difficult to define but you know it when you see it. Same with writing.

As a writer, you're trying to match words to thoughts. If you're like most everyone, you have great thoughts. Your insights into life can dazzle with depth and sizzle with brilliance. When you try to get those thoughts from your head and onto paper (or screen), though, they often emerge well off the mark compared with the original conceptions that live in the mind.

It's not that you have nothing to say. It's that you can't seem to find the ways of saying it. That's the job of revision.

Step 5: Revision

Great—you've completed a first draft. Now you're ready to "re-see" it. Maybe the writing needs only a light makeover. On the other hand, you might have produced a disaster, making your first examination of the draft more an autopsy than an analysis. A full-blown resurrection from the dead might be in order or, short of that, some serious "meatball surgery." More often, you've produced something in between a masterpiece and a huge reclamation project.

Whatever the case, no problem, because SuperRevisor, the superhero of writing, intervenes in the rescue.

SuperRevisor (that's you) can breathe life into any dead body of writing. In the worst-case scenario, you can discard that draft entirely and begin anew. As a good writer, you have attacked your assignment sooner rather than later and still have enough time for a fresh start.

A frequently recurring existential question asks: "If you could go back and change anything in your life, would you?" Most people who answer "no" either haven't thought the question throughly or are lying. I certainly would change some things. Of course, except in fantasy fiction, it can't be done, but there's one other available situation that allows this time-bending gift: Revision, the magic action that let's you go back and change the things you might have and could have expressed better but for some reason didn't.

Here are some revealing comments from writers on the importance of revision.

What Writers Say about Revision

* "If it sounds like writing, I rewrite it"—Elmore Leonard, *Newsweek*, 1985.
* "Whenever you feel an impulse to perpetrate a piece of exceptionally fine writing, obey it—wholeheartedly—and delete it before sending your manuscript to press. Murder your darlings"—Sir Arthur Quiller-Couch, *On the Art of Writing*, 1916.
* "I have rewritten—often several times—every word I have ever published. My pencils outlast their erasers"—Vladimir Nabokov in *Speak, Memory*, 1966.

* "Mostly when I think of pacing, I go back to Elmore Leonard, who explained it so perfectly by saying he just left out the boring parts"—Stephen King, *On Writing*, 2000.
* "Substitute 'damn' every time you're inclined to write 'very'; your editor will delete it and the writing will be just as it should be"—Mark Twain.
* Interviewer: How much rewriting do you do? Hemingway: It depends. I rewrote the ending of *Farewell to Arms*, the last page of it, 39 times before I was satisfied. Interviewer: Was there some technical problem there? What ... stumped you? Hemingway: Getting the words right—Ernest Hemingway, *The Paris Review*, 1956.
* "I don't write easily or rapidly. My first draft usually has only a few elements worth keeping. I have to find what those are and build from them and throw out what doesn't work, or what simply is not alive"—Susan Sontag.
* "I'm all for the scissors. I believe more in the scissors than I do in the pencil"—Truman Capote, *Conversations with Capote* by Lawrence Grobel, 1985.
* "Read over your compositions and, when you meet a passage which you think is particularly fine, strike it out"—Samuel Johnson.
* "Your rule might be this: If a sentence, no matter how excellent, does not illuminate your subject in some new and useful way, scratch it out"—Kurt Vonnegut, *How to Use the Power of the Printed Word*.
* "It takes me six months to do a story. I think it out and write it sentence by sentence. I can't write five words but that I can change seven"—Dorothy Parker, *The Paris Review*, 1956.
* "Put down everything that comes into your head and then you're a writer. But an author is one who can judge his own stuff's worth, without pity, and destroy most of it"—Colette, *Casual Chance*, 1964.
* "Writing and rewriting are a constant search for what it is one is saying"—John Updike.
* "Throw up into your typewriter every morning. Clean up every noon"—Raymond Chandler (flavorwire.com, January 8, 2013).

Becoming adept at revision is without question the hardest part of writing. You only become proficient by doing as much of it as you can, until you "get the hang of it." The more you write and revise (and read, for that matter), the more you get the "feel" for how words work well together (recall my comment earlier on the instant fix of "Vocab and Volumes"). You become adept at syntax. Keep doing it enough and you will develop a sixth sense with words similar to the instincts of a safe-cracker who can "feel" the tumblers of a lock clicking through his fingertips.

Where to begin? Before all other considerations, *don't make it worse*, similar to medicine's first rule. First do no harm. If you intervene with treatment that worsens a patient's condition, you would have been better off not doing anything. Same with revision. If you mess with your copy and make it worse, you would have been better off leaving it alone.

SWING THOUGHT NO. 10—IN REVISION, *ONLY MAKE CHANGES THAT IMPROVE THE WRITING*. NEVER MAKE A CHANGE FOR CHANGE'S SAKE.

—Never make a mark on draft copy without improving it.
—Revise as objectively as possible; be wise and ruthless with cuts and inclusions.
—Look for deadwood (DW). Cut any word that doesn't advance the text or hold its place.

Revise in a way that makes the writing clearer, sharper, more definitive and compelling, and as error-free as possible both in style and mechanics. Only revise when a change will improve the work. Never make a change without being able to justify it.

Read through the entire essay or piece, either in your head or out loud. Doing this can reveal weak areas. Reading it out loud tends to uncover the awkward parts. "Look" with your ears. "Hear" with your eyes.

Second, make note of anything that strikes you as "off key," particularly in the way of vagueness, ambiguity, awkwardness, wordiness, or illogic.

Third, ask yourself a series of questions: Did I use the right words? Do the words do what I wanted? Have I properly developed my ideas? It's one thing to state an idea. It's altogether different to fully develop it. That's the thrust of effective prose: idea-development, idea-development.

More questions to ask during revision: Do supporting materials and examples develop the CI? Do the paragraphs hold together in a unified fashion (more on that when we talk about paragraphing)? Is there any way to improve clarity? Is the material presented logically? Is anything missing? Do you need to do more research? Does the writing contain anything superfluous? Trim the fat. Just because you wrote the words doesn't mean you have to marry them. How can you say it more specifically and more simply? Do you back your claims with enough evidence? Will the reader be convinced?

I advise against having someone else read your work before you've had a fair crack at revising, especially someone who's not a good writer. Showing your work to others while the writing's still in the making leads to confusion. Too many opinions or an unqualified judgment will only mess you up, and needlessly. *You, only you,* must command your prose, part of my earlier admonition to "own your words."

I advise revising on hard copy and not on the screen. Especially for shorter pieces, print a hard copy of the first draft. Editing on screen can erase your original wordings. If you delete sections then try to rewrite; sometimes you'll find that you made it worse. Not all word processing programs will allow you to recover your original version. Using pencil rather than pen for markups makes it easier to erase. Your editing marks won't be as "final," proving a tiny but helpful psychological boost.

You'll often hear the words *revising*, *editing*, and *proofing* used interchangeably, but each performs a different purpose.

Revising

In addition to referring overall to one of the five steps in the writing process, the word also has a more specialized meaning, referring as it does to the first of three correctional actions to improve writing: *revising*, *editing*, and *proofing*.

Revision in this more limited use takes in *the big picture*, what we might call "the view from 30,000 feet." When you revise, look for large, structural problems that impede the flow and prevent the reader from "getting it," the "it" being your main message and supporting details. You're not writing for the fun of it. You're trying to communicate.

When you return to the first draft after your "walk away," consciously adjust your mindset. Pretend you haven't seen the piece before and approach it as a reader rather than the author. Step outside of yourself and see the writing anew. Strictly speaking, of course, this isn't possible, but you can achieve a good measure of objectivity by being aware of your need to do this. At this point, you're no longer a writer. You're an editor.

After you've done the overall assessment, make a gut call: What are your overall impressions? Make note of them. First impressions reveal much.

How does the essay hold together? Is all the material relevant? If not, delete the offending portions. Did you fulfill your purpose, that is, properly explain and develop your CI? Examine your paragraphs. Are they developed? Do they express single ideas? Does the draft have holes? Where? What's missing? You will have to plug those gaps. Does the work engage the reader's attention and hold their interest? Review the three major sections: Does your *beginning* create interest? Does the *middle* section develop the ideas? Does the *conclusion* wrap up the piece?

Editing

We zoom in from 30,000 feet, land, and get our hands dirty with a line edit. In a line edit, you examine each line for mechanical and technical issues, plus syntax and grammar.

How's the spelling? Is the grammar in order? Is the piece properly punctuated? Commas and semicolons aren't interchangeable. Comma usage is by far the punctuation mark that will cause the most problems. How about syntax? Do the words flow from and into each other nicely? Is the grammatical relationship clear between and among words, phrases, and clauses in each sentence? Sometimes a simple change in word order can help.

Do separate sections need subheads or section numbers? Will bullet points help present long lists more clearly? In essays 1,500 words or less, usually the answer is no. For longer work, breaking up the text might be in order. *Always keep the reader in mind.* Do anything that will make their job easier.

Check spacing. If the assignment calls for double space, give double space, not single space or space-and-a-half. Place your words on the page as if you were framing a picture. Leave even margins on top and bottom, left and right, not too wide or narrow. If font and type size aren't specified (they often are), ask if there's a preference. Times New Roman, 12 point provides a reliable default option.

Check for proper paragraph indentation. As you do this, examine each paragraph as a whole. Does it hold together? Is it unified? For nonfiction expository prose, that is perhaps the most crucial part of the entire revision process. We'll explore why in Chapter Six.

Look for the deadwood (DW)—unnecessary words. Think of your backyard after winter is over. Twigs, branches, leaves, and other debris litter the ground. This deadwood demands a spring cleanup. Deadwood lurks in every piece of writing. Like weeds in a garden, DW pops up again and again. You must make every word pull its weight. Orwell's essay referred to earlier, "Politics and the English Language," lists his "Six Rules" of writing. The third says if it's possible to eliminate a word—yes, even a single word—always cut that word. It's not unusual to find that half of your first draft is DW. You'll never find all of the DW, but a studious hunt will get most of it.

Proofing

Proofing gives one final look. Chances are, despite your most careful efforts, typos, misspellings, and other errors lurk somewhere in the lines. Find them and make the corrections, s-l-o-w-l-y, carefully, and meticulously.

You can't proof too many times. Even minutes before handing in your work, you can still make small changes to correct errors. If you're ready to hit the "send" button and zip the writing to its final destination, stop.

Proof it one last time.

Of course, with every piece of writing done on deadline, eventually time runs out. Your work becomes due and you have to let it go. Until then, consider every possible moment a chance to hunt for typos and misspellings. They love dressing in camouflage. If you don't catch them, someone else will. That's not what you want.

Finally, how do you know when you're done revising?

You're finished when you've said what you wanted to the best of your ability, having properly relayed your experience or explained the topic. Ask yourself an honest and sometimes uncomfortable question: "Did I give it my best shot?" The answer will tell you much. Then, own the work. Let the words speak for themselves. Don't be defensive or conditional when you submit a piece of writing. Words are strong. They can stand on their own. They'll fall that way, too.

Writing demands hard work, and the largest part of that labor is revision. As is the sad case with prewriting, though, many developing writers either revise inadequately or, worse, skip revision entirely. They hand in a first or lightly revised second draft thinking they've done the job. They haven't. Actually, skipping proper prewriting and revision, they've done a fraction of the work but are presenting it as 100 percent of the process. You're only fooling yourself. Your reader will know within the first two or three paragraphs, because you haven't "written" at all.

There is no such thing as writing. There's only revision.

Every piece of good and great writing that's ever been written is the product of a rewrite. Rewrites. Rewrites. Rewrites.

You can take it to the bank.

In Review

Swing Thoughts from Chapter Five.

9. You can't write a "bad" first draft because of revision.
10. Don't make changes for change's sake. Have a good reason for an edit.

Suggestions for Writing

1. Take a finished piece of your writing. Examine it with the intention of improving the copy. Revise according to the guidance from this chapter.
2. How does revision differ from editing and proofing? Discuss or write about it.
3. Take a page of your writing. Find all the DW.

Suggestions for Reading

1. "12 Contemporary Writers on How They Revise," lithub.com—The title says it all. What's interesting is how each of the dozen deals so creatively with the same tiresome-but-vital task.
2. "From Mess to Success: A Writer's Guide to Revision," writermag.com—I like this for the practical advice. You will too.
3. "Revision," writingcommons.org—This presentation calls revision "sustained thinking" about a draft. It shares what it calls a systemic approach to the oft-haphazard and vague process of revision.

CHAPTER SIX

Writing's Magic Pill: The Paragraph

It's your first day in a writing workshop. You're nervous. The presenter walks into the room and announces: "Good news, ladies and gentlemen. After years of experimentation, I have finally developed a magic pill. I'm going to give each of you one of these little beauties [HOLDS BOTTLE OF YELLOW PILLS] to take right now. Just one of these will instantly turn you into an accomplished writer. No side effects, except it will also improve your reading, make you a more articulate speaker, and give your thinking new lucidity."

Your dream come true? Too good to be true?

Well, there's good news and bad news.

First the bad news. I don't have such a pill.

The good news, though, is that I have the next best thing. Something so close, in fact, that it can do all those things the "magic pill" can deliver. I'm about to share with you the secret—*THE SECRET*—of writing effective, nonfiction, expository prose. It's been hiding in plain sight for most of your days any time you've tried to write. You know what it is or at least have heard the name. You've been using this device practically all the days of your writing, but have you been using it properly? To quote Hamlet, "That is the question."

To what do I refer?

Take a deep breath.

You sitting down?

The magic pill of writing is—is—the paragraph. Yes, the simple, unassuming paragraph.

No kidding. That humble grammatical construction can quickly take your writing ability from "X" to "X+1" or more, sometimes overnight. Learning the inner workings of this marvelous device can transform your writing more than any other single tool or tactic.

How can this be?

Let's closely look at this question, because grasping it is one of the most important lessons for any writer, especially nonfiction writers.

A paragraph isn't just any random collection of words stuffed together to make a bunch of sentences. It's something far different. A well-constructed paragraph is like a beautiful, precisely built machine. If it was a car, it would be a Mercedes or a Rolls. If a camera, a Leica or Hasselblad. That proficient machine has working parts, and, to function correctly, the machine needs those parts to come together to form a connected *unit*. Look at that last word—the root of "unity."

Concord. Connection. Combination. Coalescence. Confederation. Concurrence.

Get the point?

To fully appreciate the "how" of a paragraph, zero in on that singular concept. Here's a useful definition: A paragraph is a group of *associated* sentences that *combine* to express *one* idea. "*Associated, combine, one*"—do you see what we're driving at? Get the thesaurus. Any word that conveys "unity" gives you the essence of that incredible machine, the prose writer's best chum.

The Working Parts

The working parts of a paragraph consist of a topic sentence (TS) followed by development conveyed in the subsequent sentences. The TS states the main idea that governs the subsequent sentences in the paragraph, which flush out the idea with specifics. That's the overall pattern of expository writing. You state a general idea, then develop it with examples, details, and illustrations. State generally, develop specifically, and keep doing it until you wrap up. Too much bad writing occurs not because the writer lacks good ideas but because the ideas aren't properly developed.

Undeveloped ideas come in two general varieties, each containing numerous variations: lack of specificity and rhetorical confusion. In the first case, the writer shares the idea but moves on from it too quickly, that is, without adequate specification. In the second, the writer presents not one idea in the paragraph but two or more, often several, each lacking development. Proper paragraph construction solves both problems, like moving the focus ring on a projector to turn a blurry image into sharp clarity.

Also, keep in mind this axiom: Be specific. Writing the word "tree" lets the reader imagine the tree of their choosing, be it a birch, maple, oak, hemlock, or pine. Writing "a 30-foot blue spruce," on the other hand, creates an image. Same with "a black, 2011 Ford Focus" rather than "car."

Look at this example, the TS in bold with subsequent developmental sentences:

> **Most people today use the word "Marxist" in a political sense but have little understanding of Karl Marx, the man behind the "ist."** People forget or don't know that Marx, the restless but brilliant emigre to mid-19th century England, advocated ideas that today would be considered "capitalist." That's because 21st century capitalism no longer causes the horrible overcrowding of cities Marx witnessed in Manchester, England.
>
> **That human tragedy troubled Marx to apoplexy.** The textile mills paid poorly, requiring thousands of workers including children breaking their backs 12- and 14-hours a day, six days a week. The sudden influx of this many people led to crowded slums with little sanitation. Raw sewage caused disease, contaminated water supplies, and led either to early death or a miserable existence.
>
> **The dreary existential issues for the new working poor of 19th century capitalism are today often mistaken as an excuse to attack Marx's philosophy of private investment.** ... This TS would then be followed by the development of the CI.

The TS of these paragraphs make overall assertions. The paragraphs don't stop there and then scurry off to the next idea. Rather, the sentences that follow develop the assertions with detail. The final sentence of the first paragraph provides a great segue way into the succeeding paragraph and subsequent idea. Notice how the two are related.

So what's "magic" about a paragraph? It's *the basic unit of writing*. Look at the components of language. Going from smallest to largest, we begin with the individual letter (A through Z, 26 characters of the alphabet used to compose everything ever written in English). Next in ascending order comes the word, phrase, clause/sentence (dependent/independent), paragraph, section or chapter, and finally the finished piece.

Why among these seven items is the paragraph writing's basic unit and not one of the other six? Moving up from the lone letter to each next and larger unit like an elevator rising from the first floor in a seven-floor building, it's not until you get to the fifth floor that you find *development*. A single word or phrase contains no *development*. A sentence might hint at *development*, but, discounting rare exceptions, no true ideological evolution takes place.

Only on the fifth floor, the paragraph, do you find the general idea unfolding into specifics. These details engage readers, in effect "locking them in." Let's encapsulate this crucial lesson in our next Swing Thought:

SWING THOUGHT NO. 11: *STATE YOUR IDEAS*, THEN *DEVELOP* THEM. NOTHING IS MORE IMPORTANT THAN PROPER DEVELOPMENT.

— Nonfiction prose proceeds from the general to the specific.
— Illustrate your main ideas by providing examples.
— A topic sentence directs the reader to a specific destination.

Look at this paragraph:

> *Despite Pope Paul VI's intentions, the change in papacy caused many cardinals and bishops to fear for the council's future. Some worried that the new pope's more conservative views might cause him to cancel Vatican II altogether. After all, no schema had yet been adopted. True, Montini didn't have the outgoing personality or charisma of his predecessor, but he was above all a pragmatist. In realizing how outdated the Church had become, he left himself no other choice but to resist the reactionary elements, who did their best to take advantage of Pope John XXIII's death. The new pope met this resistance with courage, deciding the council should maintain a spirit of openness to change and allow an authentic debate to occur regarding the Church's direction. Consequently, the fear of change proved largely unfounded.*

Can you spot the topic sentence (TS)?

The TS is usually found in the first or second sentence. In our papal example, it's the first. The subsequent sentences illuminate. Sometimes the TS ends the paragraph as a kind of summation and reemphasis. Although it's not the TS, notice how the final sentence in the paragraph serves such a purpose. Sometimes, the TS is implied rather than stated directly. Nonetheless, it will always be present.

Do you see how that TS provides direction to the reader for where the paragraph is heading? The writer subtly takes the reader by the hand and leads them into the development. Readers expect that. They want the writer's thoughts stated and properly exemplified so they flow into the next (related) idea. Readers don't consciously think about all this, of course, unless the writer fails to properly develop the ideas. Then they notice the paragraph wandering aimlessly. Readers reject being led to nowhere and don't like being dropped off in a wilderness without a compass or a map.

Here's another example of a solid paragraph:

> *In the early days of the craft, photographers were viewed as wizards holding power over a dark, poorly understood force. This eerie technology produced lifelike images, exact in every detail except for color and size. Those who marveled at the photograph's power and flocked to its novelty believed they were in the presence of the sacred—or its opposite. To be sure, the pictures that rendered people and things into tiny, exact duplicates had to be voodoo or black magic. If one could exact pain by sticking a needle into a doll, what would happen if one possessed a photo of an enemy and did the same or burned it? It truly scared many folks.*

Can you spot the TS here? Correct, the first. Okay, but *why* is it the TS? Yes, because what follows *develops* the general thought.

Often you'll hear writers and readers talk about "flow." It's a great water image referring to nothing more (and certainly nothing less) than the idea-then-development dynamic. Proper development provides gravity to writing, pulling it inexorably in a smooth direction forward to its destination. Sticking with the water comparison, development gives paragraphs an undertow that pulls the reader along, pleasantly, as if on a raft.

Consider the following analogy to help you better understand how developed paragraphs relate to an overall, finished piece of prose. A TS is to a paragraph what a controlling idea (CI) is to the finished work. The CI governs the overall direction. In the same way, a TS powers the specifics for ideas to remain on course.

In developing your paragraphs, it's *crucial* not to stray to other interesting but unrelated ideas. This traps catches tons of writers. Don't fall into it, but if you do, free yourself during revision.

What if the writer had written this about Pope Paul VI:

> *Despite Paul VI's intentions, the change in papacy caused many cardinals and bishops to fear for the council's future. Montini was born in 1897 Concesia, Brescia in the Lombardy province of Italy. He had two brothers, one of whom*

became a politician, the other a doctor. He attended Cesare Arici School and in 1916 entered the seminary. …and so on.

The TS of the paragraph leads the reader to expect a certain direction. The writer, however, strays into biographical details unrelated to the paragraph opening. The material that follows the TS may be interesting and might work fine in a separate paragraph elsewhere, but here the subsequent material is out of place. As a result, the paragraph wanders, leaving the reader high and dry. If the writer doesn't fix this during revision, the reader will be confused. Here's a reliable rule of thumb: *Never introduce more than one idea with a paragraph.*

Look at this paragraph:

> *When early automobile manufacturers began perfecting their vehicles, few realized what a profound change cars would make in the American way of life. The early vehicles at the turn of the century were inefficient, expensive novelties, playthings for the wealthy out of economic reach for most Americans. Production efficiencies such as Henry Ford's assembly line, however, would change that and make reliable cars accessible to a much wider group. More families purchased cars, creating a demand for roads. This in turn opened new parts of the country for people who had essentially been hemmed in, living within the limits of how far they could walk or how many miles they could cover with a horse and wagon. America discovered The Highway and fell in love with its cars.*

The TS can be found in the first sentence. It states that the automobile changed America, which the subsequent material properly develops. Notice also how neatly the last sentence sets up the next paragraph, which will focus on the American fascination with automobiles. It's a fine paragraph, but what if it did this:

> *When early automobile manufacturers began to perfect their vehicles, few realized what a profound change the automobile would make in the American way of life. The early vehicles at the turn of the century were expensive and impractical. Henry Ford was one of the great inventors America has ever produced. Ford's ingenuity came as no surprise to his family. Even as a boy, he could be found tinkering on gadgets and taking apart clocks and compasses to see how they worked. Ford was a prototype of the "rugged individualism" that became an American archetype. There were many such people, including Thomas Edison and immigrant Nikola Tesla. Edison and Tesla were both geniuses in developing electrical technologies, but they became bitter rivals. Their legendary battles left Edison in control of an empire and Tesla a broken man who died alone in a cheap hotel room.*

Do you see the problem? This *graf* (newspaper-speak, short for paragraph) wanders all over the place. The wayward information may be interesting, but it's not irrelevant. The ideas jump around like popcorn seeds exploding with no lid on the pan. The writer starts out with one idea—the lifestyle changes induced by cars—then flits to a second (bio information on Ford), then a third (the Edison–Tesla rivalry). All three ideas lie stranded, beached castaways on the Island of Undeveloped Grafs.

When a writer tries to squeeze too many ideas into the paragraph, it's known as "rushing the development." Rushing results in scrambled writing and confused readers who soon leave you in the dust pondering what went wrong.

You don't want to do that, certainly, but you'd be shocked to find out how much it happens in writing, an occurrence that cripples prose, betrays scrambled thinking, and conveys the writer's lack of rhetorical awareness.

It doesn't have to be that way, and it never should. Let your work develop organically with the strategy we discussed: idea, then development, one unified paragraph at a time. A finished piece with this kind of solid paragraph structure creates a unified impression on the reader. It *says* something. It takes them somewhere. On the other hand, writing that hip-hops over the place comes off as incoherent, disorganized, and confusing.

The writer achieves rhetorical unity and directional definition only through *relevant* supporting material. This leads us to our next Swing Thought.

SWING THOUGHT NO. 12: KEEP EXAMPLES *RELEVANT*. THE SOLID PARAGRAPH DEVELOPS *A SINGLE IDEA* ONLY.

—Paragraphs are like little machines. Each working part has a necessary function.
—Learning the "secret" of paragraph unity immediately improves prose.
—Ideas must be relevant above all else.

Ideally, you want both interesting *and* relevant, but if and when it comes to a choice between the two, if the material strays from your general idea, chuck it without hesitation or find the proper place for it elsewhere in the piece. *Relevance always tops interesting.* Here's the formula: 1p = 1i/r (one paragraph = one relevant idea). It's as simple (and complicated) as that.

When examining your paragraphs for how well they hold together, what are you looking for exactly? Just this: A solid paragraph contains three essential qualities.

— A good paragraph is **unified**. Each sentence helps develop one idea by flushing out the details of the TS. Delete all stray material. Don't "fall in love" with the words just because you wrote them.

— A good paragraph "holds together." It's as if the period at the end of each sentence is a dot of superglue binding it to the next sentence so that the paragraph is a solid block, something like a cinder block used in construction. This **coherence** enables the reader to easily follow your thinking, winning their confidence and instilling a desire to keep reading.

— A good paragraph has all its working parts. It's **complete**. It states and develops an idea. Development includes example, detail, illustration, speculation, and fact.

Swing Thought time:

SWING THOUGHT NO. 13: A SOLID PARAGRAPH IS UNIFIED, COHERENT, AND COMPLETE.

— How "long" should paragraphs be? As long as you need to develop the TS.
— The TAB key signals the next idea.
— Be sure to properly transition between paragraphs.

A question that sometimes comes up is "how long" should a paragraph be? The answer is that there is no set answer. A paragraph should be as long as it takes to state and develop the TS. For what it's worth, the "average" paragraph of expository prose runs to about 150–200 words or so. As a rough guideline, when you look at a manuscript page typed out in 12-point Times New Roman, if you're seeing between two and three paragraphs, you're in the ballpark.

That said, there can be long paragraphs, even in published and acclaimed writing, that seem to beg for a break—a line break that is. This variation is often a matter of style. Writers such as William Faulkner, James Joyce, and Tom Wolfe would often compose long sentences and paragraphs that went on at great length without a break. Faulkner and Joyce largely wrote fiction, which is an entirely different animal. At the other end, you'll find the crisp, clipped, bite-sized paragraphs of Ernest Hemingway or Sherwood Anderson. Again, fiction writers. As a writer of nonfiction exposition, let your material and your style determine what works best for you in terms of paragraph length. Nonfiction doesn't well tolerate *The Amazing, Colossal Paragraph That Ate the World*. That's the kind of Grade Z horror that good writers avoid. In the same way, a series of short, choppy, undeveloped paragraphs cause readers nausea that makes sea sickness feel like a soothing massage.

There is also a special kind of "paragraph" used as a transition between one section of an essay and the next or to link major sections of a piece. This is the one- or two-sentence paragraph. It's called a paragraph because graphically it will be indented, but that's where the similarity ends. Such a device functions purely as a transitional signal. It's not a true paragraph at all. Sometimes these transitional paragraphs can take on a more traditional length, though they tend toward brevity. They serve as bridges rather than solid buildings. Check out Alice Walker's essay, "Beauty: When the Other Dancer Is the Self." There are five such transitional paragraphs, set in italics for emphasis.

Other exceptional "paragraphs" include lines of alternating dialog between or among more than one speaker. Each new line of dialog requires an indent, as in:

"Dan, how did you answer that critic?"

"I told him my words were strong enough to stand on their own. I thanked him for his feedback and added I neither endorse nor dispute a reader's reaction to anything I write. My words don't need a defensive perimeter to keep reactions out, be they favorable or unfavorable. They stand as is."

"That's most generous of you," she said.

Now we come to the TAB key. Yes, it deserves special mention. That TAB key at the upper-middle-left on your keyboard serves as more than just a shortcut for indenting your paragraphs the proper number of spaces. Hitting TAB to indent sends an important signal to the reader. Pressing that button tells them to expect the next idea in the sequence of the body of your work. Keep that in mind. Start a new paragraph only when you've properly developed the one you're working on and are ready to begin the next. Consequently, hitting TAB is by no means random. You do it for serious—that is, strategic—reasons.

Sometimes I get asked, "How do I divide my work into paragraphs?" Not only is that the wrong question. It's an absurd question. You don't take a piece of writing and "divide it into" paragraphs. That would imply that the writing first emerges fully-formed, like Athena from the forehead of Zeus. Writing gets done one letter at a time and does not arrive as one long, uninterrupted block, after which the writer looks at the manuscript and says, "Okay, it *looks* like I need a paragraph here." That's making the decision on page layout for "cosmetic" purposes and not for conceptual reasons. Such an approach doesn't work. You don't "divide into" paragraphs by eyeballing a long block of text. You move from one to the next based on ideas and development.

If that's clear and you begin to work your paragraphs in this way, you've already taken that next step ahead in your writing. You're at X+1.

In Review

Swing Thoughts from this chapter:

11. Paragraphs should state main ideas generally (TS) and develop them specifically.
12. Triple-check the relevance of your developmental material.
13. An effective paragraph is unified, coherent, and complete.

Writing/Discussion Prompts

1. Compose a unified paragraph on an aspect of one of the following topics: Your favorite college course, a hobby or sport you enjoy, your first job, or your first car. In one paragraph, you can't say everything. Limit your focus to one key aspect of the topic and fully develop it. *One idea only.*
2. What's the importance of the TAB key? What signal does it send to the reader? Answer in a well-developed paragraph.
3. Which sentences do not belong in the following paragraph? The sentences are numbered:

(1) The summer of Woodstock, two years removed from the Summer of Love, would soon exhaust the limits of idealistic flower power in favor of a more calamitous fascination with drugs and violence. (2) Dr. Albert Hoffman first synthesized LSD in 1938 from the fungus of a rye plant. (3) He thought he had discovered a cure for mental illness and other psychiatric conditions. (4) A Massachusetts-based band led by Mick Valenti, The Quarry, performed all three days of the festival as the house band. (5) No one played more music there than The Quarry. (6) The innocent core of gentle flower power had drawn into the mix a chaotic collection of dabblers, moochers, and hangers on—the fate of all organized movements. (7) Peace and love gave way to the destruction of drugs and violence. (8) The music of the late 60s was marked by experimentation and psychedelia, reading its peak with the release in 1967 of The Beatles' "Sgt. Pepper's Lonely Hearts Club Band" album. (9) Into young minds not ready for the seriousness of expansion, the love of the hippies turned sourly into the mayhem of Altamont, Hell's Angels, and the burnouts of Haight Ashbury. (10) The Stones were rival to the Beatles but never surpassed the "Fab Four" from Liverpool.

Answer: Sentences (2), (3), (4), (5), (8), and (10) do not fit into this paragraph.

Reading Suggestions

1. "Beauty: When the Other Dancer Is the Self" by Alice Walker—"Beauty" defines and describes this essay. Walker talks of a childhood trauma and how it ended up changing her life, first through insecurity and regret, finally through redemption as seen by her baby daughter. Walker elevates her gift for language into the poetic.
2. *The Elements of Style* by William Strunk and E.B. White—Theeeeee absolute classic stylebook, bar none. No writer should be without it.
3. *Wordsmith: A Guide to Paragraphs and Short Essays* by Pamela Arlov—This easy-to-handle book rivals Strunk and White in brevity, although its tone is far lighter and conversational. Clearly written, it includes apt readings from other writers. Geared more for the classroom than Strunk and White.

CHAPTER SEVEN

Beginning-Middle-Ending

You may have heard real estate agents talk about the three most important factors in selling a house: location, location, and location. This refers to the value of the site. An average home in a hot market often will be worth more than an upscale property in an area where few want to live. A shack in Beverly Hills will outperform a luxury duplex in a rough section of Windy City. With this in mind, let's look at the "locations" in pretty much any finished piece of writing. In it you will find four major sections of "real estate." They are:

1. Title
2. Beginning (Introduction)
3. Middle (Body)
4. Ending (Conclusion).

In writing and speaking, the three-part structure of Beginning-Middle-Ending (BME) has assumed a revered place in rhetoric. As humanity invented, developed, and refined writing systems, the need for organization became apparent. It was the only way for writing to support the intricacies of conceptual thought. The BME structure is generally credited to early Greek orators and dramatists, who dealt with the political and existential complexities of human existence. The plan since has stood the times of testing as well as the test of time.

Simply put, it's the most reliable plan for structuring a speech or a piece of writing. The funny way of describing this structure goes as follows:

Tell them what you're going to tell them, tell them, then tell them what you just told them.

In short, there's no better way to organize a work of prose than to give the reader an opening that grabs attention, a middle section that states and develops a series of main points leading to a theme, and an ending that effectively wraps it up, often by reemphasis.

Let's examine the three major sections, saving the title for last.

Beginning—The Introduction

You're at a party with a friend. You see someone you know, wave, and she comes over. You want your two friends to meet. What do you do? You introduce one to the other. In doing this, you don't tell them everything about the person. That's not possible. You say just enough for them to establish a connection and peak some interest—names, what they do for a living, where they work, their majors, where they live, where they're from, what schools they attended, what classes they're taking. You look for some common ground. For instance, maybe they both have an interest in photography or share the same tastes in music. You get them wanting to learn more about each other, and they take it from there or not.

Your writing is like that. The essay you've written is your "friend" you want to introduce to your reader who's attending the "party." You make an introduction with the idea of sharing just enough to let the two meet and pursue the relationship on their own—the writing meeting the reading with the intention of developing a mutual interest defined by close relationship.

Think about it. Readers approach your work knowing nothing but the title, which may give a hint at your topic (or may not). After that, the reader doesn't know what to expect. They enter unknown territory. You want to ease their concerns, make them feel they've come to the right place, then want to continue forward. The introduction has that job.

SWING THOUGHT NO. 14—*INTRODUCE THE WRITING* BY GIVING THE READER A HINT AT WHAT'S TO COME.

— The introduction reveals the subject and establishes tone.
— It should stimulate curiosity and interest.
— The intro establishes a purpose and creates an expectation.

A good introduction should do one or more of the following:

Reveal the subject. It can do this by stating the CI. In saying this, keep in mind that the CI doesn't have to be in the introduction though it often is, especially in expository writing. The CI, though, will be stated or implied somewhere in your work, often early.

Stimulate interest. Readers are like fish. To catch them, you need bait. The introduction provides the ideal spot to drop the lure into the water. Sometimes the intro will contain a teaser, a hook, or a "preview" of what lies ahead. Think of a movie trailer. In those two minutes, the producers try to entice you into seeing the entire film. The introduction functions as the "trailer" for your work.

Establish purpose. A good introduction foreshadows what you want to say to the reader and informs them of your theme. A writer usually indicates this through tone and the establishment of a CI.

Create expectation. Giving your reader an idea of what lies ahead in the body (middle) helps the reader ease into the piece, like slowly entering into cold water to avoid the unwelcome shock of diving in.

Imply structure. Let's say a paper begins by telling the reader that the stock market crash of 1929 had four major causes. This immediately tells the reader to expect a discussion of those four factors in the body. Or an article begins this way: "Politics is not for the faint of heart. Despite the politician's typical promises of unity, this 'great American pastime' has a long history of causing division and discord. Each era has its unique brand of politics, and a historical examination can tell us much about today." The word "historical" suggests a chronological arrangement of the material that follows.

Establish tone. A piece begins with this: "Three and only three simple rules guarantee writing at the level of the greatest master." It sets up the reader to expect a profound revelation. Now comes the punch line: "Unfortunately, no one knows what they are." This tells the reader the tone will be light and humorous. Will the paper be technical? Controversial? Will it try to move the reader into some action? Will it be funny? Sad? Will it be straightforward and strictly informational? The intro will give a taste. It should be like a pot of homemade soup. To find out if it came out right, the taster (the reader) only needs a sip to get an idea.

The introduction is the "set up" of the middle (body) of the finished piece. I use two images in trying to convey that purpose. The first is a flashlight. The reader begins reading in the dark having little or no idea of what comes next. By the time the introduction ends, the writer has turned on a beam of light that shines down into the rest of the piece. This beam of light won't illuminate everything but will illuminate just far enough ahead so that the reader feels comfortable to find the way forward.

The second image is that of a golfer placing the ball on a tee to be able to drive it long and straight. A good intro puts the body on the tee, perfectly setting up the prose to propel the reader forward.

The Middle—Body of the Writing

There's not much to say about the body except one crucial point. The paragraphs between your introduction and conclusion are where *development* takes place. Development of what? Your main ideas, each in support of the CI.

Back to the real estate analogy. For the body of the essay, the three most important words are development, development, and development. The intro sets up the piece. The ending brings it to a conclusion. In the middle *you say what you want to say*. Though you may hint and allude to it, you say it—that is, develop it—nowhere else.

In the body, the planning you did in prewriting pays off in a big way—or not in the sad event that you cut corners, for it's in that "pre" work that you align your main ideas into coherent form. Your research and brainstorming provide the specifics to develop those ideas in logical order and compelling fashion.

As we said in our discussion of outlines, once you get into the actual writing, pay attention to what happens. Staggering punch drunk, stalling, or stopping and quitting suggest inadequate prewriting. In the same way, moving smoothly along bodes well. The material begins to organize itself in a way you couldn't fully anticipate. That provides the strongest indication the writing is coming alive. When this happens, you can feel like Colin Clive's portrayal of Victor Frankenstein in the 1931 film *Frankenstein*, the iconic scene when the body Dr. Frankenstein stitched together from the parts of several cadavers comes to life.

"It's moving. It's alive! It's alive, it's alive!! Oh, IT'S ALIVE!!!"

Without question, when this occurs, the writer discovers the most important signal that they're on the right track, except that the writer hasn't created a monster that will kill but a wonderful creature that has never existed and will enlighten.

Listen to what the writing is "telling" you. Pay close attention to unexpected twists and turns, usually an indication of the piece finding its stride. It can also be that you are straying into irrelevancy. Your CI provides the litmus test.

SWING THOUGHT NO. 15—THE BODY OF THE ESSAY IS WHERE YOU SAY WHAT YOU WANT TO SAY.

— Look for the writing to come alive.
— Listen to what new developments are telling you.
— Transition into the ending to prepare the reader.

After you've thoroughly flushed out your ideas, it's time to wrap up. Be sure to transition into your ending, taking care not to slam the reader over the head with it. In other words, avoid the overused and trite "In conclusion..." or "In summary..." When the final section begins that way, it's usually a red flag, a sign that the writer isn't sure how to end it or what to say. Stay away from this unoriginal device. Include instead a transitional sentence or paragraph to ease the reader into the conclusion.

Ending—The Conclusion

The ending of a piece wraps up your case, secures loose ends, and reinforces your overall point. It's a valuable piece of "real estate"—some say the most valuable—because the conclusion is, by definition, the last thing your readers digest and take with them. That final thought provides a valuable tool with which to "win the case."

The conclusion should provide *a sense of an ending* similar to how a music composer finishes a piece of music. It can fade out in the manner of many pop songs or provide the emphatic finale as you often hear in classical music—Beethoven's Fifth Symphony, for example. Once you hear those heroic notes, you know the symphony had ended.

SWING THOUGHT NO. 16: THE CONCLUSION OF A PIECE OF WRITING SHOULD GIVE THE READER A SATISFYING *"SENSE OF AN ENDING."*

— Your ending will be the last thing a reader takes away.
— The conclusion must provide the reader with a satisfying finish.
— You can conclude by summarizing, speculating, or both.

There are two types of conclusions in expository writing (actually, three, if you count an amalgam of the first two). They are the *summary ending* and the *speculative ending*. The third is that combination, the *summary-speculative ending*.

Summary Ending

Here you finish by repeating—better still, reinforcing or recapitulating—the main points made in the body of the essay. Think of a mirror that you're placing face up, shining into the body of the piece. A summary ending "completes the cycle" of your idea, a "closing by returning."

Here's an example of a summary ending:

> *As we have seen, many factors went into the Great Crash 1929. Chief among these were overpriced equities that led to an overheated economy, too many banks making bad loans, rising debt, and lack of action by the federal government when speculators exposed the market's structural weaknesses.*
> *The shame is that few investors listened to those voices advising caution. The failure to heed good advice and instead follow the emotions caught up in a rising market caused many to suffer and set up the country for the Great Depression. The signs were there for all to see.*

The writer has returned to the main points made in the middle of the essay. This organic summary adds valuable (and memorable) reinforcement.

Speculative Ending

With this type of finish, the writer either concludes with a thought-provoking question or invites the reader to speculate on the implications raised by the topic. Sometimes, the topic and treatment allow for both. Unlike the summary ending, which points back at the body, a speculative ending directs the reader beyond what you have written, outside as it were. Here's a speculative version of the same example used for a summary ending:

> *As we have seen, many factors went into the stock market crash in 1929. Chief among these were overpriced equities that led to an overheated economy, too many banks making bad loans, rising debt, and lack of action by the federal government when speculators exposed the market's structural weaknesses.*
>
> *The shame is that few listened to the voices advising caution. The failure to heed good advice and instead follow the emotions caused by a rising market caused many to suffer and set up the country for the Great Depression. The signs were there to see, but giddy investors refused to see them or if they did, didn't take them seriously.*
>
> *Isn't it eerily similar to what the country experienced in the Great Recession of 2008? In addition, aren't the signs we're seeing today, with a Dow above 35,000 points, similar to the days leading up to late October 1929? What will an overvalued market do to the country this time around?*

In that final paragraph, the writer asks but doesn't answer three questions. This gets the reader to formulate their own responses. This directs the reader outward beyond the points made in the essay and into their own musings, a powerful strategy for a memorable coda.

Notice how both endings begin with a tip-off transitional phrase, "As we have seen …" A phrase such as this can serve as a handy signal to the reader that the writer is about to shift out of the body and bring the writing to a close. It avoids the deadly sledgehammer of "In conclusion."

Believe it or not, many writers, the bad ones, do not end their essays. Sure, they will have a final paragraph, last sentence, and the period at the end of the piece. It's impossible not to have a final paragraph, sentence, or period, but that's not the same as successfully wrapping up. If the essay just stops, it slams the reader into a concrete wall or tosses them off the rim edge of a deep canyon. The collision and the steep plunge ends in "Splat!" Not pretty, and either will leave the reader mighty ticked. You don't stop a car going 75 mph by slamming on the brake. You ease off the gas, feather the brake, and glide to a full stop. Just as in driving, you don't want the stop cold in your writing and deploy the airbags.

In sum, a good ending should:

— Arise organically from the body of the essay.
— Relate logically to the other material.
— Reemphasize the major point or points.

— Leave an impression, lasting image, or thought the reader will remember.
— Agree in tone with what you have presented in the beginning and middle. If your essay is humorous, keep the ending that way. Serious, satiric, informative and neutral, argumentative? Same thing. Be consistent.
— Leaves the reader satisfied that you have concluding the proceedings intelligently.

Dos and Don'ts for Endings

— *Do* be sure you have concluded properly. Have you given the reader the "sense of an ending"?
— *Do* convey the feeling that "It is complete."
— *Do* recapitulate the main message. Your CI will prove invaluable here.
— *Don't* introduce a new idea. That will only confuse the reader. Develop your ideas in the body of the piece. Proper revision of your first draft will reveal this problem.

Never begin a new idea in your wrap-up. This is one of writing's few "nevers."

It's a common mistake for writers who have not planned properly and probably the single most common factor in botched conclusions. They reach the end, find they forgot to include an important point or two, then try to stuff the new material into the wrap-up. It doesn't belong there.

You can't tack-on new development at the end without confusing the heck out of your readers. It may not seem like a big deal, but it is. If you begin throwing new ideas into the mix, you signal the reader that the piece isn't over. When the reader finds out that it is not "finished," an unsettling sense of confusion hovers in the air. Don't alienate readers this way.

Some Final Tips

Openings. Many find writing the opening paragraphs to be the most difficult part of writing. Such writers can't seem to begin. They look at the blank screen and freeze. Here's a proven strategy that fixes this common problem: Begin at the end. Save the opening for last. The reason is simple. As we've seen, when you begin draft copy, you can never be sure where the material will take you. How do you know what you're going to say (intro) until you've said it (body)? Only after you've gotten well into the body of the essay does your direction become clear. Once you've finished with the middle, you have all the clues you need to write an effective opening.

Closings. One strategy that cannot fail in concluding is to refer to the points made in the introduction. Here's an example:

INTRO:

> *In the maze of a big city, it's easy to get lost in the swirl of activity, the constant noise, and the throbbing pulse and pace. To the sensitive soul, it can feel like madness—organized madness, true, but madness nonetheless. If you find yourself in this situation, what do you do? Do you ignore the stress only to find it sneaking up on you at times when you least expect it, or do you take action?*
>
> *Granted, it's not always easy to make a change, but it might be the best thing you could ever do for yourself. Why not try it? Why not consider a trip to the country to slow down and dip into the placidity of nature? Why not slip into the quiet?*

The writer then develops the main idea in the body. The essay closes this way:

> *Taking the time to clear your busy schedule for some "me" time might not be easy, but once you give it a try, you could find the antidote to those big-city swirls of noise, the throbbing pulse, and the blurring pace. You can escape the madness and find all the activity you need by dialing down the decibels. Sometimes you win the race by running slowly and hear the most by slipping into the quiet.*

Let's look at another example of how you can effectively "match" an opening with an ending.

INTRO:

> *America's "Unpardonable Sin" used to be failure. Today it's criticizing the onslaught of technology that has inundated us, especially burying young people, who have been born into the high-tech tsunami.*
>
> *It seems impossible to escape the presence of screens, constantly glowing and waiting for a message to be sent or received. Social media such as* Twitter *and* Instagram *can make life easier in many respects, but common sense informs us that such convenience comes with heavy tradeoffs.*

CLOSING:

> *Having lost the free and quiet of time so characteristic of life before the screens*
> *of smart phones and social media, many have rebelled against the technological*
> *onslaught in an attempt to subdue the inescapable chatter emanating from their*
> *screens. The avalanche of technology has many advantages but, as we've just seen,*
> *it's also exacted a pricey tradeoff that many find too high to pay. An encouraging*
> *number of young people have discovered the common sense to put their phones*
> *down and to say to social media and* Twitter, *"Go tweet yourself."*

Title

Unless you strike brilliance at the outset, you should save the title until last. Once the piece is finished, a title will often suggest itself. Too many writers make titles an afterthought. Big mistake. A title should never be a throwaway. The title should assume its rightful place as a full and equal member of the three other pieces of writing's "real estate." Think of a title as carefully as you would in naming your first child.

Writers are sometimes asked to title their work. If not asked, then they should jump at the opportunity to do so. Like chicken noodle soup when you have a cold, a good title will never hurt you and can likely help. When writing professionally, usually the editor will come up with the title of a piece or—if it's a newspaper, magazine, or online article—the headline. Nonetheless, it's still good practice to include a title when you submit your work. Once in a while, they'll actually use it.

Give the title serious thought. It's the first thing your reader sees, your first chance to make a quick-hit impression. Don't waste it.

A title begins your job of "romancing the reader." Use a little psychology. Be creative. Don't just use a "label" title. When your instructor sees a title such as "Homework Response" or "Question 4," they're thinking: "Huh? That's the best they could do?"

There are two ways to title a work: Descriptive and Suggestive.

Descriptive

This type of title provides a straightforward identification of the topic such as "Chess: How to Improve Your End Game," "An Anthology of Contemporary Poetry," or "Major Causes of the Civil War."

Suggestive

What I call an *indicative* title. Such a title is mysterious, arousing curiosity and with a tease that invites the reader "inside." Titles such as "Searching for Nowhere," "When the Sky Opened," or "Burying the Dead and Others" suggest a mood. You'll often see the Internet do this: "Shocking details emerge on White House meeting" or "NFL World Reacts to Brady's Stunning Revelation." Technically, this type of "gotcha!" title is faintly descriptive and glaringly suggestive (and usually misleading). Generally, it's best to avoid "gotchas" unless they are accurate. Too often, the "shocking details" are anything but. The headline writer lured you into at least clicking on an article you would have never scanned if the header read "White House Meeting Sets Agenda" or "Brady Shares Breakfast Routine." Falling for "Aliens Land on White House Lawn" turns you into sucker bait.

Let's see how the B-M-E principles work together in an actual piece of writing. What follows is an essay that identifies much of what we've discussed in this chapter.

Anatomy of an Essay

(SUGGESTIVE TITLE) **The Miracle Has Come**
(THE OPENING, INTRODUCING THE TOPIC)

Awash in the first breezes of spring, the green spears of a crocus rise in a Disney time-lapse of memory and mind, 24 frames a second, swaying-still pictures whose "slow rapidity" creates the illusion of movement. You've seen this before. Like the hour hand of a clock, the actual plant before your eyes appears not to be moving at all, but we know it is. The hour hand moves forward 0.5 degree a minute, and tomorrow the plant will be that much taller and again tomorrow after, taller by that much. Welcome spring.

(A TRANSITIONAL PARAGRAPH ALLOWS THE OPENING TO SMOOTHLY LEAD INTO THE BODY OF THE ESSAY)

Spring brings with it a daily sense of "new," of life reawakening. It's everywhere. All you need are the senses and the good sense to appreciate them.

(THE MIDDLE OF THE ESSAY, WHERE THE MAIN POINTS ARE DEVELOPED)

First IDEA—Get ready for the miraculous. The bud and flower appear unbidden, but how welcome they are. You want wonder? The supernatural? How about the energetic, liquid work conducted by a tree as it saps into bloom? You can't imagine the inner complexity that produces such outward simplicity. The miracle remains hidden. The effect is what you see, much like a magician's trick.

To take in that same air, in that same time, affirms a pulse that runs in sync with the rest of new life springing from old, a transformation that tells us there was-but-wasn't an "old" at all. Never was. Never is. Never will be. Your breathing aligns you to the "breathing" of nature in spring. Never is oxygen as pure.

Second IDEA—"Daily" becomes a synonym of "new," and each day delivers an opportunity to enter into a novelty, one colored Celtic green and white, the color of resurrection. How can you not feel young? You simply cannot be "old" in the synchronicity of spring. You're old only if your regrets outnumber your dreams. You're old when that look to the past becomes a camping ground where you tragically pitch tent to occupy the mistakes that haunt "what was." That is a degeneration unlike spring, a dead one.

Third IDEA—Forget the past. There's too much life to be lived *now*. Don't waste it on being "old." Inhale the redolence of linseed oil saturating the palm of an old baseball glove. That's spring, when the baseball diamonds come alive with chatter and play. Look upon the light, *lux*, streaming through the translucent handle of a screwdriver. Walk on campus. See young lovers stroll hand in hand, lost in each other like entwining vines.

Fourth IDEA—Watch the birds come back. They take wing, flutter, build, accept, and abide. They use their lives as instruments of song beyond thought but contained in awareness so holy that not one of them has ever needed to compose a prayer. Not one of them presumed to build a church or worry about a collection plate. Let the Abrahamic "Holy Weeks" come again and again, pretending resurrection lies in the rituals and incantations. Follow the animals into sacredness.

(A TRANSITION INTO THE CONCLUSION) In the final account, what can satisfy us?

(CONCLUSION) Not politics, deceits, or insults. Not apologies, means, or ends.

Then what, exactly?

How about the gazing love of anything innocent, anything not human? How about the first green spear of a crocus in spring? How about the miracle of nature? If that's not enough, I can't think of what could be. *(AN ECHO OF THE OPENING)*

In Review

Here are the Swing Thoughts from Chapter Seven:

14. Your introduction gives the reader a *hint* at what's to come.
15. The body of the essay is where *development* of the CI takes place.
16. The conclusion should provide the *sense of an ending*.

Writing Prompts

1. Write an introduction for an essay on one of these three topics: "The cinema of Stanley Kubrick," "Why texting is hurting/helping the English language," or "My high school years were (choose one) a great time in my life/wasted years that I'm glad are over."
2. Discussion—How long should the middle of the essay, the body, be? Defend your answer.
3. Write an ending for one of the three writing prompts in Question 1. If you feel ambitious and want to "go for the burn," write the entire essay. It will do you good.

Reading Suggestions

These essays follow the classic B-M-E structure. Read them and try to determine the location of these three pieces of "real estate."

1. Gary Shteyngart, "Sixty Nine Cents"—Shteyngart describes his awkwardness when his Russian immigrant family goes to McDonald's for a meal. Great example of how daily, so-called ordinary experiences often furnish the best material.
2. Lynda Barry, "The Sanctuary of School"—A young girl steals out of her troubled home at night and goes to the only place where she's not invisible. She walks alone to her school. There, a kindly janitor and a caring teacher transform her life.
3. Clara Rodriguez, "What It Means to Be Latino"—Rodriguez writes about the challenges of being the "outsider" in such a way that transforms a well-worked theme into penetrating freshness.

CHAPTER EIGHT

Transitions: Getting from "Here" to "There"

Generally speaking, when you find reading to be some combination of easy, enjoyable, effortless, or even-keeled, usually the writer has followed the principles discussed in this book. It's not because I invented anything new or made any startling discoveries that stunned the literary world. Rather, I stood on the shoulders of all the writers who came before me, selected the best elements of style and rhetoric, applied them in practice, and reduced them into a system for teaching others.

One of the most important of these selections and reductions has been a device common to all good work but one that doesn't receive enough attention. I refer to the *transitions* that move readers along and through the piece from beginning to end. We've touched on this connective device already. It's time now to move transitions (TR) onto the front burner. If active verbs form the engine that powers writing, TR provide the oil that lubricates the parts of that engine.

Have you ever noticed that when you enjoy reading how the sentences and paragraphs flow seamlessly from one to the next? Probably not, because if the writing has that type of easy movement, you're not aware of it. Same with punctuation. When the reader notices, it's almost always for the wrong reasons.

Good TR do not call attention to themselves. They are the "silent partners" in the business of prose, keeping the reader's attention on the words and through them to the writer's ideas. Proper transitioning provides the reader with immense assistance. Well-transitioned writing seems effortless and purrs along like a perfectly tuned motor. In this way, proper transitions help assure steady forward progress in the writing.

The only time a reader realizes much of anything about TR is when they are not there, for instance, a piece of information that pops up out of nowhere, with no rationale or context (recall my earlier remarks about the importance of relevance). You might begin to read something and stall. You can't get past the first few paragraphs or pages. Reading becomes too arduous and you give up. Why is that?

For a reader, tough sledding can be nothing more than disinterest in the topic, and bad writing will scare you away every time. Often, though, the answer lies in the lack of TR when a writer's main ideas shift haphazardly from one to the next for no good reason and no apparent pattern, for it is certain that when a writer gets lost, so will the reader be placed blindfolded in the woods at midnight.

Transitions contribute to coherence throughout sentences, paragraphs, and the entire piece. They do it by sending clear signals to the reader, much in the way traffic signs and red, yellow, green lights direct drivers about upcoming conditions on the road and how the driver should respond. Such signs and signals indicate what the driver should expect and do. That's how TR work. They give indications of what's ahead (or sometimes what you left behind). This is the binding function of transitional devices, one of writing's early-warning systems. By that I mean that when you do not properly transition your thoughts, your prose begins to light up with warnings that something's amiss. In the same way, when you properly transition, you provide readers not early warning but early security, settling them down with an injection of confidence in your work.

It's virtually impossible to find a piece of good writing that does not effectively transition in, out, among, and through the ideas. To this end, I used to perform a kind of "parlor trick" with my composition students, audiences, and workshop attendees. After setting it up with a spiel on TR worthy of an emcee at a Friar's roast, I'd select a someone, ask them to pick out a book, any book, and start thumbing through the pages.

"I guarantee that we will find TR. In fact, I'll pay everyone in this room $100 if we do not."

At random, I'd say to my assistant, "Stop!" then ask them to choose the left or right page. After that, I'd direct them to the first full paragraph on the page. Using a computer connection to project the paragraph so everyone could see and read it, together, I would point out the transitions. Invariably, there would be a number of them.

Here's an example of my writing. I chose it at random because it happened to be in a file on my desktop:

Someone unfamiliar with Catholic practices once asked me, "What do I do before the Blessed Sacrament?"

"Do? You 'do' nothing," I answered.

"What do you mean, 'nothing'?"

"Just that."

*To believing Catholics, the Blessed Sacrament represents Jesus incarnate. You sit before it, empty your mind, let go of the chatter and noise with which we bombard ourselves, and sink into the God within and without, similar to Eastern meditation. Actually, we can only say what God is **not**, not what God "is." Violating what I just said (for religion is the one field of inquiry that not only should accept but encourage, even demand, contradiction), "God" is everything—all universal matter and energy—everywhere, without differentiation, the Everything of All. The Blessed Sacrament acknowledges this in a special way, "reducing" the "Everything" of "is" into that single point, an ordinary piece of bread encased in a transparent holder. It does this to accommodate our limited human senses, perceptions, and awarenesses of whatever "God" might or might not be.*

The selection is loaded with transitions. I won't go through them all, but as we shall soon see, every pronoun and repeated word functions transitionally. Also look how such words ("Actually") and phrases ("Violating what I just said") connect the ideas and grease the skids, moving the writing along as if on a conveyer belt or placing the reader on a toboggan for an enjoyable ride.

This leads to our next Swing Thought:

SWING THOUGHT NO. 17: TRANSITIONS (TR) BRIDGE WRITING, ESTABLISHING *CONNECTIONS* THAT ENHANCE UNITY AND FLOW.

—"Choppy" writing often stems from improper transitioning.

—Don't assume the reader will automatically pick up on your next idea. Readers aren't psychic. You have to signal your shifts.

—TR, like all writing strategies, help the reader more than the writer. You already know where you're going. Your reader has no such knowledge.

"Connect."

That's the key word.

Not Two but Four

It has long stuck me as odd that so much writing instruction fails to emphasize the importance of TR. If they do tell you about TR, they typically mention only two. There are, in fact, four transitional devices. Without being familiar with your writing, I can confidently state that you have some in your work. The question is, do you have enough of them and in the right places?
The four TR devices:

— Transitional words and phrases
— Repetition of keywords

These are the two that get the most mention, but there are two more:

— Use of pronouns
— Transitional sentences.

Let's take a closer look.

Transitional Words and Phrases

A writer employs such words and phrases to connect ideas in a sentence, sentences in a paragraph, and one paragraph to the next. Here's a list of some common TR words and their function:

— TR, to alert the reader that an example will follow: *for instance, specifically, for example, namely, another.* Look at these examples. The TR expressions are in bold face.

For instance, a roster will undergo many changes throughout the season.
Specifically, the lighting in this scene suggests a three-dimensional effect.
　　When workers scrub graffiti off the wall, **for example,** they just invite other "artists" to go to work.
　　The "third Stooge" in the act was played by four different actors, **namely,** Jerome "Curly" Howard, Sam "Shemp" Howard, Joe Besser, and Joe De Rita.
Another reason the Alamo fell was the sheer strength of the Mexican army, which outnumbered the Texans 15-to-1.

— TR, to make a comparison: *similarly, in comparison, not only, but also.*

As it happened in World War I, the World War II allies **similarly** rallied to turn the tide.

In comparison, the Triumph's smoother down-shifting made it a favorite on the sports-car circuit.

Not only did Palmer's gallery contribute with vocal support, **but** some **also** contributed underwriting costs for the tour.

— TR, to show contrast: *however, though, although, but, on the other hand, while.*

In the fourth quarter, **however,** the Zephyrs rallied to take the lead.

Other TR can serve dual functions.

Though shopping in a "bricks and mortar" store can be inconvenient, at least you can physically handle the goods before purchase.

Although the girls' team received less attention, they outperformed the boys in the won–loss column.

The penny-candy store has faded into the past, **but** Paoli seems determined to bring it back.

On the other hand, putting your money in the bank rather than equities offers FDIC protection.

Buddin came in **while** Runnels came out.

— To indicate sequence or addition: *first, second, third; finally; moreover; also; in addition; next; then; after; furthermore.*

First, grease the pan; **second,** assemble the ingredients; **third,** preheat the oven.

Finally, the barrage ended.

Moreover, the fun run brought out a record number of participants.

The mix **also** included a cute, cuddly Beagle named Chubby.

In addition, the latch had been sheered clean off the door.

Next, make sure you keep accurate score.

You will drive 1.3 miles **then** take the second left.

After the gold rush ended, Lame Deer became a ghost town.

Furthermore, the evidence couldn't be plainer.

Repetition of Keywords

This TR device, while used less frequently than other TR words and phrases, none-theless (note the TR word I just used!) serves as an alternate connective function.

Consider this paragraph, with the repeated words in bold face:

> *I approached the **story** neutrally, with the simple determination to go where the **facts** led me. My goal was to shine sunlight on the **story** of a man **run** down and nearly killed by a hit-and-**run** **driver** who left the scene prior to police arriving. For more than a month, local media suppressed the near-death of that unfortunate pedestrian. I would investigate the **driver's** actions behind the wheel and let the **facts** speak for themselves.*

Notice how the repeated words bounce back and forth, "echoing" each other. The reader won't notice this connective effect while reading (unless overdone), but the impact registers at some satisfactory level of awareness, however faintly. The one caution here would be not to overuse repetition. Sparingly employed, repeated words connect. When overused, however, they annoy the reader or even induce sleep.

Use of Pronouns

Ironically, the use of pronouns is the most overlooked TR device but the most frequently used. A pronoun renames another noun to avoid numbing repetition such as:

> *My mother cooked breakfast for us most every morning. My mother made sure we were fed before going to school. After school, my mother picked us up for the drive home. My mother loved us like a "TV mom."*

You laugh at this, but you'd be surprised at how much of this literary anesthetizing takes place, knocking the reader out cold. How about substituting "she" for some of the "mothers"?

One of the stumbling blocks with pronouns involves the grammatical term "case." What is case? It's the relation of a noun or pronoun (formally called a "substantive") to other words in a given sentence, often shown by inflection or its position in the sentence. One notorious example is the confusion over the "I/me" pronouns. Look at this sentence:

> *Aurelio and me saw the incident.*

Is "me" correct? No, because it cannot connect with the verb. True, it's one of the subjects of "saw" but "me" doesn't properly relate to the verb. The test is to take the two subjects separately: "*Dave* heard him; *I* heard him," not "Dave heard him; Me heard him."

"Me heard him" might be fine for Bizarro in Superman comics but not for the writer.

How about this one?

Such dancing delights her and I.

You okay with "I?"

No? Correct!

Typically, we follow "you and" with "I," but in this case the two are objects, not subjects. "Such dancing ... delights *you*." "Such dancing ... delights *me*."

The clue for settling such thorny issues lies with the verb. Find the verb. It might be hiding behind a conjunction or another verb. It could even be understood rather than expressed and not physically be there at all. Whatever—find the verb.

Who versus *whom* ranks up there as an irritant to hot vichyssoise or too-tight underwear. Too often, the writer ends up guessing, but writing should involve as little guesswork as possible. The decisions made by the writer should be strategic, done for a reason and with a justification. In deciding on *who/whom*, again, look for the verb, then decide if the pronoun must be its subject, object, or predicate complement. Example:

The man whom they believed to be keeping score left the stadium early.
Whom?

No. *Who* is correct. Find the verb: "left." The pronoun takes the same case as verb.

"*Who* left" rather than "*whom* left," as in "The man *who* ... left the stadium early."

Example:

Incorrect: *Whom do you suppose left the water running?*
Correct: *Who do you suppose left the water running?* The phrase "do you suppose" does not affect the case of the preceding pronoun.

We vs. *us.*

Find the verb, as in this example:

The women in the First Division are actually younger than us.

Is *us* correct?

No. Ask yourself to what word is the pronoun related? Answer: the verb *are*. The correct for is "*we are*" rather than "*us are*."

When you see a pronoun, you can be sure that an antecedent came before it. The antecedent is the word to which the pronounce points back, thus creating a TR effect. When you revise, look carefully at the antecedent, making sure it agrees in number with the pronoun.

Look at this example:

> *At work, Pete wore a uniform that reminded us of a clown costume. It had garish colors and a funny hat that didn't fit his head.*

Can you spot the first antecedent–pronoun combination? There are three.

Yes: "Pete/his." Then "uniform/It." Notice now "he" and "It" refer back to "Pete" and "uniform." In this usage, "that" functions as a pronoun, referring to "uniform." In other sentences, the word "that" can be a definite article, a conjunction, an adjective, or an adverb. This combination of "back reference" of pronoun-antecedent creates a connection, something like a stitch that binds fabric together. The effect is subtle but effective, since it helps with coherence and unity.

Transitional Sentences

Sometimes a writer signals a dramatic shift in topic with the use of sentences whose sole purpose is to convey the reader from one major section to another. Such sentences are usually indented as paragraphs. You'll recall I addressed this earlier in our discussion of paragraphing.

A TR sentence or paragraph bridges one section to the next, showing how the sections relate to one another and giving the reader a "passport" for safe passage on the crossover. The TR sentence(s) can begin another line, indented, as you would a bona fide paragraph. It can also be placed at the end of a paragraph where it leads smoothly into the next. There's no hard-and-fast rule for this. As always with such discretionary matters, let your material decide what to do. Good writing will do that, as in the cliché of the work "coming alive." This phenomenon refers to how a well-organized, clearly crafted piece builds a critical mass that creates momentum, a direction that the writing "prefers" by being its only logical way forward. When that happens, you as a writer are said to be "in the zone."

When the writing performs as it should, it will "talk" to you in a form of communication far beyond what the actual words objectively convey. That's an aspect of writing's mysterious part, the one that can actually take it into the somewhat spooky realms of art. This is a whole new dimension that separates good writing from great. It's fine and even advisable wanting to elevate writing into this exotic realm. It can be and is done. This desire, though, must be tempered with a sobering dose of realism. No matter how good a writer you are, certain conditions, contexts, circumstances, and subjects simply preclude greatness.

A good example would be author Kurt Vonnegut. Long before he wrote his masterwork, *Slaughterhouse Five*, he worked as a writer for General Electric in one of the company's advertising, sales, and promotion offices (ASPO). Later, when reflecting on his experiences there, he said words to the effect that writing about the virtues of a new and improved power transformer offered little chance for the Nobel Prize in Literature. However, he was quick to observe, the mundane subjects given to him as ASPO assignments didn't preclude good writing, a lesson learned when he majored in journalism at Cornell University: present material based on fact in clear, direct, straightforward sentences. Never were light bulbs and transformers conveyed any better in prose.

A side thought occurs here. Nonfiction places certain strategies off-limits. Be aware of them. If, for instance, you write a nonfiction piece about Custer's Last Stand, you can't have him miraculously surviving. A fiction writer not only can do that but can go far beyond the nonsensical. If a novelist writes about a transport beam from a hovering but invisible alien spaceship sending Custer to an outdoor yoga class on April 16, 2023 at Clinton Square in Syracuse, N.Y., you can't really argue about it.

Here are some examples of TR sentences that the writer either tacks on to the end of a paragraph or TABs them with an indent indicating a new "paragraph":

— *The tour wrapped up on a high note, but everything was soon about to change.*

This alerts the reader to a dramatic shift that's about to come. The two main clauses (a **compound sentence**) perform the linking function. The first clause refers to what has previously been stated. The second indicates a shift in the writing's future direction, a classic TR.

— *So much for the easy work. To the platoon's dismay, boot camp turned into something entirely different.*

The first sentence (a **simple sentence**, that is, one independent clause) of this example implies the finish of a section detailing the "easy work." The second sentence (a **complex sentence** consisting of one dependent and one independent clause) signals the reader that the writer will shift to explore the "not so easy."

— *It's one thing to say the right words but quite another to do the right thing.*

Here we have another **complex sentence**, consisting of an independent clause followed by a dependent clause linked by the coordinating conjunction "but." Again, the TR signals a shift.

Writing without proper TR results in jumpy prose. The words take on a bad case of the jitters. It reminds me of driving a car with a manual transmission and grinding the gears because you didn't correctly depress the clutch pedal. It produces a cringe-worthy effect, the old "fingers scratching a blackboard" sound that classroom clowns used to annoy their mates, to say nothing of the teacher.

Look at this paragraph. The TR are in bold.

> *Manager Dick Williams gave the ball to a part-Cherokee Indian, left-handed rookie Billy Rohr, **who (pronoun)** would be making **his (pronoun)** first major league appearance. Most **managers (repetition of key word)** wouldn't start a **rookie (repeated word)** so early in the season, **but (contrast) Williams (repetition)** was a gambler. **Rather (shift)** than playing it safe, this skipper played to win.*
>
> *__In high school at San Diego (prepositional phrase)__, hometown of Ted Williams and Dave Morehead, **Rohr (repetition)** won 26 and lost only 3. The **26 wins (repetitions)** included four no-hitters. **After (sequence)** high school, **Rohr (repetition)** signed with the Pittsburgh Pirates, **but (contrast)** the Bucs lost interest. In 1963, the Boston Red Sox drafted **him (pronoun)** in November, a whirlwind **that (pronoun)** left **Rohr (repetition)** with a quick education in the cold-hearted business of baseball.*

The passage contains 16 TR devices. They seem obvious in highlights, but when you're reading, you don't notice. That's what you want to happen, because it means the writing is proceeding smoothly. Now consider that same paragraph without TR. Read it out loud. Hear the grinding gears? Feels the blackboard shivers down your back?

Here's another paragraph. Locate the TR and note how they work:

> *Small cars reveal the action of driving by letting you not just see but also feel the road. Move a compact hunk of metal, plastic, and glass 80 mph down the road, and you will feel it. That's why I don't like the chloroformed comfort of a large car with all the options. You get little feeling of the road, a depressed sensation of*

movement even when you hit 90, the luxury stereo sounding as if you are in a concert hall. In a large car, you lose all sense you are driving. You might even make a phone call, text, or surf the "net".

Do you love large, luxury cars run by computers? Congratulations! You have just realized the scariest yet most commonplace terror of the Age of Technology. You are in the hands of The Machines, without which your life would not be the same, as complete, or as socially viable. Give me liberty. Give me small. Give me my Mini.

A word now about conjunctions. As the word suggests, "conjunction" attaches sentence parts to each other. **Coordinating conjunctions** join independent clauses. There are only seven: *and, but, or, nor, for, so*, and *yet*.

Subordinating conjunctions join independent clauses to dependent ones. These words have the power to reduce otherwise independent clauses to dependent status, as in this example: "The sun rose at 5 a.m." The clause stands perfectly well on its own, but look what happens when you add a subordinating word: "Although the sun rose at 5 a.m." You've created a fragment.

There are about 50 subordinating conjunctions in seven categories. They include such words as *after, although, as, because, before, even, if, inasmuch, in order that, just as, lest, now, once, provided, provided that, rather than, since, so that, supposing, than, that, though, till, unless, until, when, whenever, where, whereas, where if, wherever, whether, which, while, who, whoever, why.*

Consult any good handbook for more about conjunctions.

Two quick examples:

*He's a master carpenter, **and** he has practiced the skill for 25 years.* (Coordination)
__Although__ he never went to college, he's considered an expert in his field. (Subordination)

Transitional strategies also can make the relation between two thoughts clearer. I call these Semantic Transitions.

— Semantic TR needed in this sentence: *The Chinese have spent billions on improving infrastructure. They want to expand economic development to rural areas.*

— Add a semantic TR to connect to two thoughts more logically to improve conceptual clarity: *The Chinese have spent billions on improving infrastructure, **because** they realize economic growth will depend on developing rural areas.*

— Semantic TR needed to improve the connection between two thoughts: *Trash heaps piled up on the sidewalk. The owner of the house takes good care of his property.*

TR added: *Trash heaps piled up in the sidewalk,* **even though** *the house owner* **otherwise** *takes good care of his property.*

Transitions illustrate the point we have been making through this book, that good writers try to do everything they can to make their work readable. They focus on the reader and have reasons for the rhetorical choices they make. Effective use of TR provides cues and clues to readers, ultimately injecting finished work with coherence and internal logic. As coins of American mint tell us: *E pluribus unum*—"Out of many, one." I submit that slogan as a definitive description of good writing. Out of many words, one overall theme or statement.

In Review

Here is the Swing Thought in Chapter Six:

17. Transitions (TR) supply connections between ideas expressed in and among sentences, paragraphs, and finished works, giving writing logical coherence, unity, and flow.

Writing Prompts

1. Take a page of your writing and identify the TR. In a couple of paragraphs, comment on your findings about your use of these connectives.
2. How do TR devices "smooth over" prose? Find examples taken from published articles and make your own informal study.
3. Research and compile a more complete list of TR expressions than the ones listed in this chapter. Make the list a part of your writing "toolbox."

Suggestions for Reading

In the following selections, pay particular attention to how the writers weave in and out of the main ideas using TR.

1. Alice Walker, "In Search of Our Mother's Gardens"—Another Walker classic as she artfully blends her main ideas with expert transitional effectiveness.

2. Richard Wright, "The Library Card"—In the Jim Crow area of the South where the author came of age, African Americans couldn't legally obtain library cards. Wright lets the reader in on how access to a library card opened him to a world of new ideas and filled him with rage at the discrimination he endured.

3. Lynn Peril, "Do Secretaries Have a Future?"—In this ironic, satiric op-ed column, Peril notes how secretaries, now called "Administrative Professionals," might be joining the iceman and the office boy as obsolete, rendered unnecessary by technology. Superbly transitioned.

CHAPTER NINE

Grammar and Punctuation: Accidence and Analysis

Did you glance at the title of this chapter? Accidence has nothing to do with falling off a ladder or spilling red wine on the white rug. It refers to that part of grammar dealing with inflection, the relational changes in words (for example, inflections that create a word's tenses). I chose it for that meaning and also because I liked the alliterative rhythm when paired with "Analysis." Writers use every trick they can.

Grammar refers to the guidelines, directives, and conventions that determine how a language holds together and works as a system. This chapter will review some of the more common grammatical issues and pitfalls that catch writers. The grammar being shared here refers to the standards of SAE (Standard American English, discussed in Chapter Four) to assist readers in making the decision to employ SAE as opposed to another non-SAE dialect.

The Inner Workings of Language

In teaching grammar, too much jargon and technical jumbo-mumbo hurts more writers than it helps. Good writers tend not to be overly concerned with the "verse and chapter" of grammar. You don't have to know the labels. You *do* have to know how to properly apply the grammatical elements to which the labels refer.

Grammar consists of conventions incorporating the structure of a language. These protocols form the general regulations for syntax, morphology, inflection, agreement, tenses, pronunciation, semantics, and much more. One look at that definition, however, might put you off your toast.

Here's my definition: Grammar describes how language works. This applies to SAE, AAVE, and any other English dialect. In fact, it covers all languages. No one knows the exact figures for how many languages exist in the world, because some habitable areas (such as remote parts of New Guinea) remain unexplored. Ethnologue, published by SIL International, has catalogued 6,909 world languages. This doesn't include the various dialects within each of these. Every one of them has its own grammar.

One should never learn grammar for grammar's sake. You learn because it supplies "best practices" that over time has been proven reliable. In other words, grammar is important because it works. Some call the directives of grammar "rules," but they aren't cemented in place as all that. Grammar refers more to the literary guidelines that have been adopted over the decades.

The cultural directives differ for each society, getting adopted not because of the theory behind *why* they work but because they in fact *do* work. The theorists, academics, and researchers jump in *ex post facto*, usually too late to be of much practical help.

A convention describes the best and most acceptable way to conduct an activity within cultural norms. For example, let's say you are dining at a restaurant in America. The purpose is to feed yourself. You could achieve that by eating with your hands. In some cultures, that's permitted, even preferred. Doing this in the West, though, will earn condemnation. It might even warrant a call for the cops. In our culture, you eat by convention using utensils—forks, knives, and spoons—in a quiet, considerate manner.

Grammar is similar to that. When writing formal prose, you would no more ignore the "rules" of grammar than you would enter a fine restaurant and stuff food in your mouth using your hands and fingers. Readers won't look at your work if you're too sloppy with writing's grammatical practices. If they do give your work a glance, they won't take it seriously. They'll laugh you right out of your prose.

Some History

Over the 10th through 21st centuries, grammatical structures have changed dramatically. Slowly, readers and writers figured out there might be a better way to derive meaning out of written words. Writing before the year 1000 had almost no punctuation at all. How the times have changed.

Historians and tradition credit French ruler Charlemagne (742–814) with a key role in starting the modern-day system of punctuation. He strained so much to make out the scratchings on official court documents that he began to insert marks on the texts. Where a sentence seemed to end, he would place a little dot. His reputed invention of the period (.) rivals that of the wheel, the discovery of fire, and the fame of the Kardashians. Soon, more people began to follow the practice. Over the years, more marks and inflections were added, making reading easier and more "user friendly."

As settled as you think the English language might be, in fact many linguists (Noam Chomsky and J.R.R. Tolkien, for example), communications theorists (Marshall McLuhan), and cognitive specialists (B.F. Skinner) have worked tirelessly to understand language expression and comprehension. This doesn't include countless scholars in academia who have taken a crack at linguistic nuance in piles of unread PhD dissertations. Theories of communication have been helpful to some degree, but, truly, do you think you need to study Adaptive Structuration, Symbolic Introductionism, or Frame Theory?

Fluidity characterizes the English language, which is constantly morphing. It's important for writers to understand these transformations and how they affect writing, for example, texting's impact on formal prose.

This book doesn't examine present-day linguistic theories because that's not my purpose. Current linguists (Matthew Dryer, Raenna Fowler) continue the work, trying to penetrate deeper into the inexhaustible mystery of words. Reading into these areas can't hurt, but in pragmatic terms, working writers primarily care about effective conveyance of ideas. They use computers and writing apps such as word-processing programs, but they don't care about *how* they operate. All they care about is that they *do* operate. Same with language.

Writers want to avoid grammatical errors for one simple reason. Each mistake you make shakes the confidence of your reader, and that's the last thing you want to do. Don't rely too heavily on online grammar checks. Such tools are okay but only up to a point, for two reasons. First, grammar-checking software (ProWritingAid, Grammarly, WhiteSmoke, Ginger Software, and others) is, unlike spellcheck, too often inaccurate. Compared to spelling, a relatively cut-and-dried process, grammar's intricacies are too complicated even for computers to provide consistent and reliable direction. Online grammar "correctors" often identify "errors" that are anything but—false possessives, for example, or recommending incorrect contractions and faulty usage. I can't tell how many times I've seen "you're" (contraction for "you are") incorrectly changed to "your" (possessive case). Other common frustrations include unwanted cursor jumps that hinder typing; limited vocabulary; inserting anticipatory, predictive text that makes no sense; mistakes with special characters; punctuation errors; and unresponsive buttons.

Second, relying on computers to replace organic knowledge is rarely good strategy. Having software making decisions doesn't work well in writing. Just because the computer says to make a correction doesn't mean it's what you should do. Writing is intensely individual, and the complexities of language's nuances still outdistance computer programs, which is why good writers know grammar organically and not mechanistically or through smart-aleck apps.

Sharpen Your Appetite

Actually, what a writer needs to know about grammar can be reduced to one sentence. I'll soon reveal that incredible sentence.

While a writer should be hungry to learn grammar, a few basics will suffice for most writing, making the process less intimidating. In turn, that can sharpen your appetite to increase your knowledge of what you are doing and why. Grammar and punctuation each have their own specialized language, and it will help to learn as much of the jargon as you can.

If you go into medicine, law, the trades, the military, or most any other specialized activity, you'll have to learn the jargon. Same with writing, though not to the same extent. For example, the English language has eight parts of speech describing the function of words that make up sentences. Consider the word "tie." As a **verb**: *Tie the anchor knot to the mooring.* As a **noun**: *He wore a tie for the occasion.* As an **adjective**: *The tie-dyed shirt glowed with vibrant colors.*

Knowing grammar and punctuation will help prevent the three deadly sins of writing: **fragments (FRAG), comma splices (CS), and fused sentences (FS).** All three involve punctuation errors stemming from ignorance of grammar. If you can learn to avoid these three mistakes, you're well on your way to grammatical sufficiency and the writing instantly jumps into a higher level of quality.

Before I get into the details of these three "fatal" errors, let me share the most important sentence you'll ever hear about grammar, to which I earlier referred: *All grammar stems from an ability to instantly recognize subjects and verbs.* Learn how to do that, and everything else falls into place. Try to chisel our next Swing Thought into the granite of memory:

SWING THOUGHT NO. 18: A WRITER'S MOST IMPORTANT GRAMMATICAL SKILL IS BEING ABLE TO *RECOGNIZE SUBJECTS AND VERBS.*

— Grammar is communication etiquette, a convention one observes.
— Knowledge of writing mechanics helps prevent serious technical flaws.
— Prose predicates itself upon subject and verbs.

I used to call that Swing Thought "Valenti's World Famous 10-Second Grammar Course." I had a simple reason for the jest: Recognizing subjects and verbs forms the basis of most of English grammar's other rules. Knowing how to locate these two necessary elements of the sentence will help you troubleshoot problems with sentence structure, particularly with FRAG, CS, and FS.

Grammar's Direction. In its most basic form, the English language proceeds linearly from subject (performs the action) to verb (the action performed), as in:

— *Larry (S) ran (V) the race.*
— *The Founders (S) believed (V) a constitutional republic would best serve the fledgling nation.*
— *Owens (S) possessed (V) the ability, but she (S) lacked (V) the motivation.*

Of course, not all sentences will be that direct, but basically, that's the pattern, a subject performing an action indicated by a following verb.

More examples of subject and verbs:

— *The Crunch (S) produced (V) a flurry of action in the third period.*
— *At one time, doctors (S) made (V) house calls.*
— *The agency (S) offers (V) companies an affordable alternative to in-house booking, but it's (S and V, contraction for "it is") not always reliable.*
— *With his discovery of Cubism, Picasso (S) abandoned (V) traditional one-point perspective. This innovation (S) allowed (V) multiple perspectives in two-dimensional canvass.*

You might be wondering about the difference between a "verb" and a "predicate," words often used interchangeably though they aren't the same. Unlike a predicate, a verb is one of the eight parts of speech. It can require an object (receiver of the action), making the verb transitive, or it may not need a receiver (completer), in which case the verb is intransitive. The predicate, on the other hand, is not a part of speech but a word group (verb phrase) that makes an assertion about the subject. Look at this example:

The flowers bloomed. Here, "bloomed" is the verb.
The flowers bloomed after I added fertilizer. The predicate is "bloomed after I added fertilizer."

In the following examples, notice how many words follow the *S* and *V*. Writers who can't pick out subjects and verbs will fish around for them and not get a bite. They start guessing, and that's how and why most FRAG, CS, and FS occur. In writing, a good general guideline is "Never guess. Always have a reason or strategy."

There can be more than one subject and verb combination. Look up in a grammar text the definition of "sentence types." Briefly, a **simple sentence** has one subject (which may be compound) and verb:

John, Paul, George, and Ringo (compound subject) *comprised* (verb) *the Beatles.*

A **compound sentence** contains two or more independent clauses:

The Beatles (S) made (V) their American debut on Feb. 9, 1964, and that night more than 73 million people (S) watched (V) the band perform. Each clause can stand alone.

A **complex sentence** has one independent clause and one or more dependent clauses:

While the group (S) occupied (V) an entire floor at the Plaza hotel, thousands of fans (S) gathered (V) outside. Because it begins with a subordinating conjunction, the first clause is dependent.

A **compound-complex sentence** consists of two or more independent clauses and at least one dependent clause, as in:

The Beatles (S) left (V) New York and they (S) flew (V) to Florida, where Epstein (S) inserted (V) a couple days off from their crazy schedule. The first two clauses are independent. "Where" subordinates the third clause.

Your head spinning yet? Relax and breathe.

Cherry Picking

If you can learn how to "cherry pick" the *S* and *V* from any sentence, you will go a long way to grammatical improvement.

Subjects (nouns) and verbs are two of the eight parts of speech in the English language. The others are:

— Pronoun (substantive)
— Adjective and adverb (modifiers)
— Preposition and conjunction (connectives)
— Interjection (words that show emotion, such as "wow, hurray, ha-ha." They are informal, usually punctuated with an exclamation point and *should be used sparingly*. To that point, it's generally better to understate than to go over the top. Special emphasis should be just that, special. Choose moderation over excessiveness).

Verbs are action words powering the engine of writing. Verbs comes in two "voices." Voice determines if the subject of a sentence performs the action (active voice) or receives the action indicated by the verb (passive voice). Use active verbs as much as possible to convey strength and power. If I had written this passively—"Strength and power are conveyed by active verbs"—it would be a weak construction. When overused or incorrectly used, passives come off as weak, trite—even anemic.

— Weak passive verb: *Your notes were much appreciated by the class.*
— Strong active: *The class greatly appreciated your notes.*
— Weak passive: *The tornado was seen by the storm watchers.*
— Strong active: *The storm watchers saw the tornado.*

Passives provide cover when writers wish to hide the initiators of action, as in "The controversial measure was supported by a majority of the board." Writing this instead of "Talbot, Chaney, and Lawrence, the board majority, supported the controversial measure."

When revising, pay particular attention to the verbs. Here's a helpful exercise: Print out a hard copy of your work, highlighting the verbs in each sentence, then analyze. Did you employ enough actives? Does the writing contain too many passive verbs ("is/are, was/were," and the "to be" verbs often indicate overreliance on the passive voice)? If so, revise using the active voice where appropriate.

In some sentences, verbs have helpers—words like *be, have, do, shall, will, ought, may, can, must, might, should, could, would*—called "auxiliaries." In the sentence, "He should have been watching," the verb combination (predicate) contains four words. "Watching" is the verb proper. The other three are auxiliaries.

Let's look in more depth at the three most common (and serious) grammatical mistakes: fragments (FRAG), comma splices (CS), and fused sentences (FS).

Fragments

A FRAG is a fake sentence, a series of incomplete words presented as an independent clause when it's no such thing. The fragmented "sentence" lacks a subject, verb, or both. It fails to make a complete statement; it's a dependent clause. FRAG also occur when a subordinating word introduces an independent clause. In prose, a dependent clause cannot "stand in" for a complete sentence. Stylistic fragments, the kind that dot the work of great writers, are the exception. Stylistic fragments *have to be earned*. In my professor days, 99.99 percent of sentence fragments in student work occurred because of faulty grammar and certainly not for artistic reasons.

Look at this example:

— *The secretary opened the day's mail one letter at a time. Ripping open envelopes and placing the contents in the appropriate baskets.*

The first statement is complete. It has a subject ("secretary") performing an action ("opened"). The second is a FRAG. Neither subject nor verb are present. The noun, "secretary," doesn't carry over to the clause that follows. Moreover, "Ripping" and "placing" are not verbs but *verbals*, constructions formed from verbs but used as either nouns or modifiers. Here's the sentence revised:

— *The secretary opened the day's mail, ripping open envelopes and placing the contents in the appropriate baskets.*

Replacing the first period with a comma provides the fix, with "ripping" and "placing" acting as nouns. Unlike actual verbs, verbals don't take a subject. There are several other ways to correct the fragment. As always, let your material and context decide on the most effective fix.

One of the best ways to identify a FRAG is to read it out loud and ask: Is this a complete thought? Does it "sound" okay? Can it stand on its own? Often you can hear the FRAG. Of course, as we saw earlier with subject–verb recognition, it's better to identify them on sight.

Read this passage from one of the sample paragraphs introduced in Chapter 6. Identify the FRAG, if any:

> *(1) In the early days of the craft, photographers were viewed as wizards holding power over a dark, poorly understood force. (2) Exact in every detail except size. Even those who marveled at photography's power believed they were in the presence of the sacred—or demonic. (3) Many actually feared the process. (4) Early photos were formal, posed as much as exposed. (5) The blacks, whites, and ambers. (6) Rendered objects into tiny duplicates of themselves. (7) It had to be voodoo. (8) If one could exact pain by sticking a needle into a doll, what would happen if one possessed a photo of an enemy and did the same?*

The fragments are sentences (2), (5), and (6).

Is It a Sentence or a "sentence"?

When you write and especially revise, examine the sentences. Does each contain at least a subject and finite verb (a verb that agrees with its subject and indicates proper tense)? If so, you have a complete sentence.

Read this passage. Are both clauses independent?

> — *John loved to spend his money as fast as he made it. Especially when he had cash at hand.*

The first sentence passes the "completeness" test, but what of the second? It has a subject ("he") and a verb ("had"), so why isn't it a sentence? Answer: It's introduced by a subordinating conjunction, "when." This instantly reduces what would otherwise be an independent clause to dependent status. The majority of sentence fragments in developing writers stem from this dynamic.

Here's a list of common subordinating conjunctions.

> *after, although, as, because, before, how, if, since, than, that, though, unless, until, when, whenever, where, wherever, while.*

A subordinate clause is a group of words containing both subject and verb but introduced by a subordinating word. The subordinating words function as a single part of speech, thus subordinating the "sentence" to follow.

Examples (subordinates in bold face):

— Subordinate clause as adjective: *The musician* **who practices the most** *will achieve the greatest mastery.*
— Subordinate clause as adverb: *They will go* *where we go.*
— Subordinate clause as noun: ***Wherever you travel,*** *they shall honor your presence.*

Comma Splices (CS)

Comma splices have the dubious distinction of being the most frequent serious grammatical flaw of developing writers. Commas in general cause conniptions, far more than any other punctuation mark, mainly because some are discretionary.

A splice joins two objects, for example, two pieces of film. Electricians often have to splice two wires together to establish connection. A CS occurs when two independent clauses are linked only by a comma. Instead of establishing a connection, a CS blows a fuse, such as this sentence:

The pavers sealed the driveway, it has made the yard easier to plow.

To repeat: A CS joins (splices) two sentences that actually function independently. They can stand on their own as independent clauses.

As you can see, a comma isn't strong enough by itself to link two complete sentences.

The test for determining a CS is simple:

a. Locate the linking comma.
b. Cover the comma and read the clause to the left. Can it stand alone as a complete thought?
c. Do the same, reading the clause to the right of the linking comma. Can it, too, stand alone?

If the answer to b. and c. is yes, you have a comma splice. A comma alone is not strong enough to link two independent clauses.

There are four fixes. Which one you choose depends on the nature of the CS in question and how the repair fits stylistically.

Fix 1. Remove the comma and replace it with a period.
Fix 2. Replace the comma with a semicolon.

Fix 3. Link the two clauses with a coordinating conjunction, of which there are only seven: *and, but, or, for, nor, so, and yet.*

Fix 4. Keep the comma and demote one of the main clauses to dependent status with a subordinating conjunction (mentioned earlier).

CS—Fix 1

Remove the comma and replace it with a period, the simplest correction. Let's apply the fix to our example:

The pavers sealed the driveway. It has made the yard easier to plow.

A word of caution: Don't write too many simple sentences, especially consecutively. This will put the reader to sleep faster than sleeping pills. Vary your sentence structure. It's like a major-league baseball pitcher. No matter how fast he throws, he needs more than a fastball. If that's all he has, hitters will figure it out. Good pitchers command at least three or four pitches. Same with writing. Good scribes command different sentence types.

Some quick tips on introducing more sentence variety:

— Change the length.
— Vary the beginnings.
— Avoid too many of the same sentence types in a row, especially the simple type. Use a mix. Different lengths change the "timing" of sentences.
— If appropriate to the material, slip in a pertinent quote or a rhetorical question.
— Don't barrage the reader with too many adjectives or adverbs. It makes for bloated writing.

Back now to our remedies for repairing CS.

CS—Fix 2

Replace the comma with a semicolon.

The pavers sealed the driveway; it has made the yard easier to plow.

Note how the semicolon sets up a stronger relationship between the clauses.

Writers, drill this into your head: *Don't overuse semicolons* as indiscriminate substitutes for periods or to replace linking commas. Moreover, *commas and semicolons are not interchangeable.* Use semicolons when you want to join two main clauses that have close conceptual relationship to each other. The semicolon turns the clauses into "twins." Compared to a period, a semicolon implies greater logical unity between the clauses.

CS—Fix 3

Link one clause to the other by adding a coordinating conjunction. This gives equal weight to both independent clauses of a compound sentence.

> *The pavers sealed the driveway, and the yard became much easier to plow.*

CS—Fix 4

Keep the comma, and subordinate one of the clauses.

> — *After the pavers sealed the driveway, the yard became easier to plow* or *Because the pavers sealed the driveway, the yard became easier to plow. The first example conveys a logical "given" between the two clauses. The second version creates a cause-effect relationship between the clauses.*

A subordinating conjunction placed at the beginning of a main clause immediately "reduces" the clause to dependent status.

Fused Sentences

A fused sentence (FS), sometimes called a run-on sentence, occurs when two or more independent clauses have a head-on collision. This occurs when the writer places no punctuation between complete thoughts.

> *At the museum, the visitors stopped before getting to the gem exhibit museum staff had roped it off from the public.*

You need a period. Where? Right. After the word "exhibit" then capitalize the "m" of "museum."

Here's another one: *The volleyball tournament drew all levels of competition Sandy entered the Intermediate Division.* Yes, the writer needs punctuation, either a period, semicolon, or a comma with conjunction to link the phrases.

When you isolate an FS in this manner, it appears obvious, the proverbial sore thumb plus bruised index finger and black eye. Maybe you're asking, "How could I write something like that? If I scribbled something like that, I'd surely catch it."

Yes, one would think, but I can't tell you how many times otherwise decent writers present finished work with FS. This indicates either that they revise and proof carelessly (if they do it at all) or they don't recognize the fusion.

When you write and revise, you must do so *fully engaged.* Most FS stem from simple carelessness. Be deliberate in your work. Focus. Write precisely and revise meticulously. Don't rush anything. By the way, is the above word "Focus" complete or a FRAG? I put a period there. If it's an independent clause, where's the subject? If you answered that it's complete, you win the prize. In the **imperative mood** (also called mode), the subject "You" is understood. In grammar, "mood" telegraphs the writer's attitude toward the subject, also called tone.

The **imperative mood** issues commands, orders, or instructions: *Go out and play to win.*

The **indicative mood** states or declares, asks a question, or denies an assertion, as in *The children shouted* (declaration) or *Are you actually going to wear that?* (question) and *No, you weren't listening* (refutation).

The **subjunctive mode** expresses uncertainty, makes a wish, or states something contrary to fact. Subjunctives sometimes can be identified by their typical use in dependent clauses beginning with *that* or *if*. Examples: *Who's to know if Thomas chose correctly or not* (uncertainty)? *I hope the game goes well* (wish). *If I work on my essay rather than go to the party, I'll get a better grade* (contrariness).

Even as you improve your writing, you might find these and other gremlins sneaking into your work. Humans aren't computers, nor do we possess perfection. Mistakes will occur. Fine—as long as they occur in draft form and not in the finished work.

Make note of any grammatical issues that feedback identifies. Make the effort to understand the "why" of grammatical mistakes. As your work progresses and you become more adept, you should notice a dramatic drop-off in the frequency of technical errors.

SWING THOUGHT NO. 19: KEEP A *RUNNING LIST* OF ALL GRAMMATICAL AND PUNCTUATION MISTAKES

— Make note of your errors. Try to understand why they have been flagged.
— Don't take feedback personally. Constructive criticism is a writer's gold.
— By far the comma will give you the most headaches. Give comma usage special attention.

When someone flags grammatical issues, ask "why?" Why is that a CS, FRAG, or FS? You should be able to answer. If not, ask for help. Do that with any grammatical notations. Eventually you'll get the hang of it, because writers tend to repeat the same mistakes. Good critique will identify errors, and over a significant sample of your work, you'll notice the same problems being flagged. That's the supreme value of expert review. If you're not getting competent feedback, ask for it.

Another important point with respect to critiques: Never take criticism personally. Writing is so intensely personal that many writers develop a phobia about sharing their work. Rather than risk scrutiny, they shove their manuscript into the desk drawer or lock it inside a computer file. If you have such a problem, do whatever it takes to get over it. To be a serious writer, you need to develop a thick skin and maintain a positive attitude. Writing loves sunshine. Recall our earlier declaration to "own your work." Give all assignments their due, putting out all that you have, and then "owning the work." Don't be defensive. That's not to say you should have a chip on your shoulder, although I have often thought that a great headspace for a writer should be the thought that they have *two* chips, one on each shoulder, for balance! Own the writing by letting the words stand on their own.

Briefly, let me mention some other common faults:

— Problems with case. Case involves pronouns, which must clearly refer to the correct antecedents. "You and I" versus "You and me" is a good example of case.
— Word problems. *Homonyms* are words that sound the same but have different meanings and spellings. Learn to use them correctly: there, their, and they're; your and you're (most troublesome); bear and bare, affect and effect, very and vary, do and due, it's and its (contrary to what some "writers" believe, the word *its'* doesn't exist).

Spellcheck won't help. Run this sentence through spellcheck: "*Your the only won who affectively completed they're assignment.*" It will not find a single spelling error—because there are none. The problem in this sentence comes with the homonyms "Your," "won," "affectively," and "they're." For misused homonyms, spellcheck is useless.

Proper nouns must be spelled correctly. *Faulty compounds* such as any where (anywhere) and no where (nowhere) needed to be corrected. *Typos*: If you type "live" but meant "love," spellcheck, again, is useless.

— Faulty subject–verb agreement.
— Use of incorrect tenses. Know when to use present (He skates), past (He skated), future (He will skate), present perfect (He has skated), and past perfect (He had skated). Stay consistent in tense throughout the piece.

Mastering the science, craft, and art of writing takes a lifetime, but progress is well within your reach, right now, as you are. You only need to want it, then go to work.

Here is an exercise for you to practice with FRAG, CS, and FS.

In the following passage, underline any sentence that's grammatically incorrect and state why. Sentences are numbered. Answers follow the passage. Don't peek.

(1) Price's book analyzes Robert Wise's adaptation of Shirley Jackson's horror classic, The Haunting of Hill House. *(2) He reviews the film scene-by-scene to show how* The Haunting, *Wise's version, lifts Jackson's book out of the confines of the typical "horror story." (3) Into an examination of a descent into madness, shown by Julie Harris' portrayal of Eleanor Lance.*

(4) This transforms what would have been mere "genre" film-making into a classic, the film has been widely praised by critics. (5) Despite critical acclaim, however, there has not been a book on this film prior to Price's, an absence that has been long due for correction. (6) He taught this movie in film classes for many years he says recent student responses to this 1963 masterwork tell him the film is still entertaining and scary.

(7) The book contains interviews with Richard Johnson ("Dr. Markway"), Julie Harris, Claire Bloom ("Theo"), and Russ Tamblyn ("Luke"), they add new insights into the film. (8) The best "ghost film" ever filmed. (9) Other features include an index that helps readers compare novel and film, many production stills, and a compendium of reviews.

Answers: Sentence three (FRAG), four (CS), six (FS), seven (CS), eight (FRAG). How did you do?

Punctuation Proper

While making it easier to share instant communication with others, texting has had a detrimental effect on writing that needs more structure and expression. Make sure your texting habits do not infiltrate your formal writing, particularly sloppy punctuation. Writers can object all they want about this reality, but they need to accept it. That's how the business of writing works. If you wish to gain respect as an author, even if it's just an office memo, you must elevate writing to a more structured, mature level. The instantaneous nature of texting simply does not suit the needs of the classroom, business, editorial offices, and other situations requiring elevated prose.

When you need to write more formally, pay special attention to punctuation. For example, on a job application or writing a report, don't get sloppy. Even when texting a friend, it's a good habit to mind the details. It will help your writing stay in good technical shape and keep you from bad habits.

The basic punctuation marks include the period, comma, semicolon, apostrophe, and special marks (dash, quotation marks, parentheses, brackets, colons, and ellipses). Punctuation marks are like the symbols used in musical notation, directing how the material should progress. Punctuation exists solely to help the reader. My favorite analogy is to liken punctuation to traffic signals and signs.

— **Period, exclamation point, and question mark**: A red light. You must come to a full stop.
— **Comma**: Slow down, not a full stop, something like a "Slow, Curve" sign with an arched arrow.
— **Semicolon**: A stop or yield sign, depending. Come to a full stop and proceed if it's safe. Think of a semicolon as a comma on steroids. The semicolon—;—graphically consists of a period placed directly over a comma. A semi has the power of a period to stop a main clause but only if it doesn't end the sentence. It has less power than a period but more power than a comma. *Commas and semicolons are not interchangeable.*
— **Special marks**: Marks such as exclamation points and question marks indicate inflection and how the sentence should be read. Use exclamations *sparingly* and only for surprising declarations.
— *He walked to the cabin* (a straight declaration) is a far different sentence than "*He walked to the cabin?*" (suggests incredulity) or *He walked to the cabin!* (amazement).

Comma Usage

Writers invariably find commas the most vexing peculation mark, and too many writers guess. That some commas are discretionary only adds to the confusion. Guessing never provides a good reason to do much of anything with the written word, let alone add or omit punctuation. You always want a reason for doing (or not doing) things. That separates a "guess writer" from a strategic writer.

Use a comma to:

a. separate introductory phrases
b. separate main clauses in a compound sentence linked by a coordinating conjunction
c. set apart nonrestrictive word groups
d. separate items in a series
e. enclose parenthetical elements within a sentence

That's only a partial list. There are several other comma uses, and a good handbook will explain them. I've listed the ones that are likely to cause trouble. Let's look more closely.

a. *Introductory phrases*: If your sentence begins with a word, phrase, or subordinate clause before the subject, use a comma to set it apart.

Examples:

Despite the dense fog, the planes were able to land safely.

When breaking in a new baseball glove, oil it properly.

> *With his hands gripping the wheel, Jack steered the car into the narrow space.* For brief introductory elements, the comma can be discretionary: *Obviously there is much work remaining before we can begin construction. Consequently the movements after the adjustment featured greater fluidity.* You don't need a comma after "obviously" or "consequently," but insert one if you think it will help the reader. I tend to put them in because, as a reader, I find them useful. A comma after an introductory element will never be incorrect.

b. *Separating main clauses*: When you use a coordinating conjunction to separate two or more main clauses, place a comma *after* (*not before*) the final word prior to the conjunction.

Examples:

The will left everything to the staff, and the children received nothing.

The invasion went as planned, but establishing a beachhead proved difficult.

Sometimes, writers will inexplicably place the comma after the conjunction, as in:*As a resort, Elmwood leaves much to be desired although, the menu is superb.* (The first comma separates the introductory element from the main clause. The second comma should come after the word "desired").

c. *Setting off nonrestrictive modifiers*: Such a modifier isn't crucial to the meaning of the sentence. It can be removed without destroying the main idea, but the writer includes it for a more complete meaning. Set apart such modifiers with commas.

Examples:

Jeannie's eyes, which were blue, matched the sky.

The foreman's report said Bedell, who couldn't keep pace, would not be promoted.

Compare these cases to clauses considered inseparable from the noun:*The foreman said workers who were industrious would get raises.*What would you do with the following sentence?*George Smith who is the hardest worker in camp deserves a raise.*Correct. Commas needed after "Smith" and "camp" because the person has already been identified. The meaning needs no restriction. Now this one:*Workers who give 100 percent effort deserve promotions.*What do you think, commas or not? Right. No commas here. The general term, "Workers," needs further identification. And this:*The knee that was hurt has completely healed.*No commas. The clause needs restriction, because there are only two knees.*Parilli, who hurt his right knee in the season opener, came back in the fourth game.*Yes, commas set the nonrestrictive element apart. The team has only one Parilli, and the man has two knees.Loose modifiers such as appositives are detachable clauses and phrases. Appositives are nouns or noun-equivalents placed beside other nouns or equivalent expressions. They need to be set off, such as:*H.L. Mencken, an outspoken writer, is considered by many to be the greatest prose stylist of the 20th century.*When the modifying clause or phrase is "built-in" or modifying so closely that you can't separate it, it is restrictive and does not need commas:*A nation that has an authoritarian government generally lacks concern for human rights.*

d. *Use commas to separate items in a series (called a serial comma)*: Examples:

The Stooge lineup most fans prefer consists of Moe, Larry, and Curly.

The army invaded town, looted stores, then moved to the next hamlet.

The children were behaved, polite, and happy.

Some style books recommend eliminating the comma after the penultimate item (second to last). I strongly recommend keeping that comma there. Doing so will help avoid confusion. Consider this series: *The recipe called for a mix of flour, shortening, sugar and butter.* Is this a series of three or four items? It can be read both ways. Adding a comma (after the word "sugar") avoids this uncertainty.

e. *Use commas to separate parenthetical expressions.* Such phrases add information, confirm, or explain.

John Goswell, Union Federal Manager, presented his lineup to the umpire.

Murdock, an agricultural community in Missouri, has seen a decline in family-owned farms.

The goal, my friends, is to improve last year's totals by 10 percent.

In the end, grammar is the most elemental yet most complicated aspect of mastering writing. If you keep at it, improvement is certain.

In Review

Swing thoughts from Chapter Six:

18. The most important grammatical skill is the ability to recognize subjects and verbs.
19. Keep a list of all errors pointed out in feedback.

Writing Prompts

1. What punctuation mark gives you the most trouble? Discuss or write about it.
2. What is your attitude toward formal writing versus texting? Explain in a solid, unified paragraph.
3. Do you think texting and social media have helped or hurt your writing? Put your thoughts into writing.

Reading Suggestions

1. "Why I Write" by Joan Didion—The great prose stylist shares thoughts that will help most any writer, from novice to pro.
2. *The Blue Book of Grammar and Punctuation* by Jane Strauss—A no-nonsense presentation of what too often becomes a sticky quagmire of grammatical fastidiousness. Strauss keeps you on solid ground.
3. *The Only Grammar Book You'll Ever Need* by Susan Thurman—I Like Strauss's book but more so this one. Thurman has a knack of turning the learning of grammar into a painless situation. Like getting anesthetized before dental work, Thurman makes what is usually an unpleasant task tolerable.

CHAPTER TEN

Making Your Case: The Rhetorical Modes of Exposition

Broadly speaking, the entire universe of the English language can be divided into two categories: prose and poetry. That's it. By definition, anything that isn't poetry is prose, a word that references ordinary, everyday language of accepted, common, cultural usage excluding most slang and some aspects of the irregular vernacular. Prose comes close to the patterns of everyday speech and writing. Unlike poetry, it isn't primarily metrical. Meter certainly is present in prose, but not in the assertive sense that it is in poetry.

Consider the meter of these two sentences conveying the same meaning, the first in prose, the second in poetry.

Prose: I stopped by the woods to look at the trees, but I wasn't sure about the owner's name.

Poetry: Whose woods these are I think I know. (Robert Frost).

Hear the difference?

When you write for your courses, work, a writer's group, or professionally, you're swimming in the pond of prose, communication rarified and filtered from speech by the differences between talking and writing. Talking (and texting) spew forth, often spontaneously and not fully thought out. Imprecision and errors are expected and easily overlooked. Writing, however, elevates words to a more lofty status through deliberation and revision into a more polished, finished form.

Prose further divides into two categories: fiction and nonfiction. Fiction is writing that springs from the author's imagination, presented as "fact" in the figurative creation of worlds and situations meant for readers to take as "real" through the willing suspension of disbelief. You can think of a million examples: the *Star Wars* and *Twilight* series, the *Harry Potter* books, the great books of fictive literature, or any movie you've seen that's not a documentary, even (especially?) those "based on true events." Usually, fiction strives to make a point through an established theme, an invented plot, and created characters. That theme is often what we used to say about Aesop's Fables and Grimm's Fairy Tales, the "moral of the story."

Nonfiction springs from facts based on actual events and experiences. Nonfiction entails greater care for accuracy, and it generally involves some aspect of reporting that we can think of as expository. Genres include history, biography, psychology, sports, travel, science, and so forth. True, you can incorporate the techniques of fiction into nonfiction—dialog and interior monologues, for example—to great effect, but essentially in prose you will be a reporter and an interpreter, not the creator of an imaginary world. Fact and reasoned opinion will be your domain. Ironically, nonfiction has it harder, since the writer's reportorial and interpretive version of incidence and circumstance—"reality"—will never conform to the actual event it's trying to depict. The worlds and realms of fiction, on the other hand, exist only as the author portrays them. They cannot be anything other than what they are. This applies even to historical fiction given the reader's willing suspension of disbelief.

Nonfiction further produces two types of writing: *expository* (from the root word "expose") and *argumentative* (also called *persuasive*; I'll explain the difference later in this chapter). Expository prose has one purpose: to inform the reader. Argumentative prose seeks to do that plus one more thing. In addition to informing, argumentative prose presents an informed opinion and tries to persuade the reader to agree with the writer's point of view. Not all expository writing is argumentative, but all argumentative prose is expository.

Take any controversial topic, abortion for instance. No doubt you will find a variety of strongly held views ranging from "Abortion equals murder" at one end to "Abortion deals with a woman's inherent right to control her body" at the other, plus all points in between. A strictly expository piece on abortion will "expose" the reader to a descriptive view of the topic, presenting, for example, numbers, various state laws restricting or permitting, federal and state mandates, data, methods, legislation, grassroots activism, and other such facts—even the politics of the issue providing the writer presents them even-handedly and not ideologically. The writer won't take a position on the moral aspects, though they may be presented informationally.

An argumentative piece on the same topic, however, will state a point of view, defend it, and seek to convince the reader of the soundness of that view, up or down. It will be written in a calculated attempt to provoke or assuage one side or the other with respect to the writer's position on the topic.

In writing for your courses or nonacademic assignments such as those that come to you in the workplace, you will be asked to produce your share of non-fiction, expository prose. Sounds intimidating, but as you continue to develop as a writer, you will be armed with a process, the one explained in this book, that enables you to produce good writing *on demand* by *deciding to do so*. Your main purpose will be to provide information and perhaps tell a story to illustrate a point. In prewriting, you assemble your controlling idea (CI) and supporting information, state them in words as best you can, then revise. The process goes from general statements to specific illustration, all leading to a central point.

If your employer asks you to write a description of your job duties, you will write a "how to" as a sort of training manual. The CI is built into the task. Or say you have to write about an abstract concept such as the word "hero." How would you handle it? You might then combine description, example, narrative, and definition to tell the story about the squad leader who dove on a grenade, smothering the explosion with his body and sacrificing his life to save the others in his command.

There are many rhetorical forms that, used alone or usually in combination, help the writer achieve that goal. They include:

Description
Example
Narration
Comparison and Contrast
Cause and Effect
Process Analysis
Definition
Classification and Division
Argumentation and Persuasion.

In the remainder of this chapter, we'll briefly examine each of these with special attention given to argumentation and persuasion.

Rhetorical Modes

By far the most important and frequently used of these techniques are Description, Example, and Narration. They are present in nearly every form of expository prose.

The Big Three

Description: This is the journalistic 5Ws + H design—who, what, when, where, why, and sometimes how. Follow that newsroom formula, and your descriptions will provide the essentials. Description is spatial, detailing the physical features of an object, place, person, animal, or thing. Except for the most experimental writing, perhaps, it's near impossible to write prose without heavy use of this technique. Don't go overboard, though. The trick is to provide enough details so the reader can "see" the object, situation, person, or place, excluding extraneous details. Often it helps to depict the view from a logical perspective such as top to bottom, inside and out, an overview from far off, then to closeup, and so forth. Your CI will help you decide what to include and what to leave out. In other words, when describing a subject, don't "take inventory." That's where the writer includes too much extraneous material and tries to describe everything. It can't be done. When it comes to writing, even one worthless word is one word too many.

"Taking inventory" when describing is an easy trap, one that snares many writers. You could write 100,000 words on what you ate for breakfast, but would you want to? Perhaps you would if you were James Joyce writing about Leopold Bloom on June 16, 1904, but you're not James Joyce, are you? The lesson: When describing, don't take inventory. Include only the *relevant* details. Every word must pull its weight. I once had a writing instructor tell me to pretend every word I wrote would cost $10. At that rate, one tends not to waste words. And remember Orwell's third rule from "Politics and the English Language:" If it's possible to cut a word, do it.

Example: Exemplification provides specific illustration to flesh out general points—the essence of expository prose. It's the essential flow of expository prose, first to establish a generalization then to follow up with representative examples. Almost all writers have the ideas, but you'd be surprised at how many writers overgeneralize, that is, state the idea but do not develop it with examples. Exemplification supplies the ideas with specificity, creating images the reader can see. For example, let's say you write a topic sentence: *A recording studio resembles the control panel of a spaceship.* The rest of the paragraph had better provide details, mentioning such specifics as dials, switches, illuminated panel lights, readouts, microphones, cables, inputs, outputs, and the like. Fail to do so and guess what? Your reader just pulled the ripcord to bail out. If you state "The U.S. postal service is unreliable," you'd better be sure you give examples (lost mail, delivery to incorrect addresses, slow service).

Narration: Where description is spatial, narrative is chronological, which, incidentally, is why they complement each other so well. Literally they present the subject in both space and time. Narration tells a story, a "this happened, then that happened, followed by the next thing." Time order ("Once upon a time...") provides a convenient organizational pattern. Begin at the beginning and take the reader through the story as it unfolded over time. Yes, one can "time machine" a story with dips into and out of the past and future, but that's tricky and best left to the fiction writers. Keep it simple. One reliable pattern is to begin with a teaser, then set up either the story's conflict or rationale. Every story must have conflict in the form of a problem or difficult situation that must be overcome. From there, resolve the conflict and end by sharing the "moral" or lesson. Narrative makes a point, which supplies the reason to share a story in the first place. If I tell the story of how I learned to swim at summer camp, the overall point would be: "Face your fears or they will eat you alive." Every good narrative does this. Readers often come with a built-in affinity for narrative, since storytelling is a form of conveyance that has appealed to them since childhood. Think of the books your parents read to you as a child, if you were so fortunate.

The Others

In support of the Big Three rhetorical techniques, several other writing patterns can help convey your ideas with prevision, provision, and precision.

Comparison and Contrast: This special form of analogy compares a familiar with the unfamiliar for the purpose of illustrating an idea. If you write, "Raising a child is like growing a garden. Both need feeding, watering, and loving care," you have two things that on the surface have no relation except for the common point that both need care and attention. It's the same with this simple comparison: "Churchill fought like a provoked lion." Both were ferocious. Comparison notes similarities. Contrast details differences.

Cause and Effect: Cause asks the question "why?" Why did the machine fail? Why did the house catch fire? Why did Mike make the team but not John? Why did the plane crash? Effect asks "what if?" What if the stock market tanks? What will happen to the economy? What if we put Lagroterria in for Packard? Will we play better? What if America hadn't fought the Civil War? How would that have changed the country's future? As an expository technique, cause and effect can be most illuminative. There are two kinds of causes, immediate and ultimate or underlying. The immediate cause of the fire might be faulty wiring. The ultimate cause would be the failure to have it properly inspected or cutting corners because of money pressure. Note that each deeper "cause" is also an effect. The fire started because the homeowner did the job herself, didn't get it inspected, and cut corners, all to save money. She need to save money because of credit card debt. The debt had a cause, and logically and literally, you can trace everything back to the Big Bang or Creation by Design, whichever you prefer. The point is to trace cause and effect back but tempered with common sense and reason about where to stop the chain of evidence. Three things must be present for a causal relationship to exist. First, the cause must always precede the effect (time order). Second, as the cause is introduced, the effect occurs (concomitant or sympathetic variation). This, you must rule out of other factors (Z variables).

Process Analysis: A "how-to." Process refers to a set of instructions presented in a series of steps, usually in order, leading to a desired outcome. Any food recipe is a common example of process analysis. Many other examples abound: how to put together a table, a job description, how to light a cigar, how to change the oil in a car, how to baby sit, how to avoid trouble with the IRS. The trick to a good process lies in breaking down the action into separate steps, taking care not to omit any and including advice on what to do if things go wrong.

Definition: Objective definition (denotation or literal meaning) you find in the dictionary. Subjective definition (connotation or associative meaning) conveys the *feel* of what you're defining. Example: You can define "beer" as a consumable beverage brewed with water, malt, and hops. It can't get more objective or literal. If you define beer as your "feel good tonic" or "happy juice," however, you're conveying an inner or subjective definition. Subjective analogies can let the reader in on the emotions of an experience, such as Joan Ackerman's engaging description of watching the Space Shuttle blast off at night. She loads the essay with subjective definitions using lots of figurative language, for example, likening the booming, burrowing noise of liftoff to the pounding of a bass drum felt vibrating inside your chest cavity. The image resonates on an emotional level. Subjective description best gets at the essence of the object. You can describe a baseball as a white, circular object weighing 5.25 ounces, with a 9.25-inch circumference, a 2.8-inch diameter, with a cover fastened by 108 double-stitches. You could also say it's the color of all colors, white, that when put into play triggers a pastoral game dating back to the Civil War, a game now out-of-place in today's world of blurring pace and speed.

Classification and Division: When you take a subject consisting of multiple parts and place them in categories, you're classifying. When you take a subject considered as a single entity and break it down into component parts, you're dividing. Putting knives, forks, and spoons into their separate spaces in the drawer *classifies* the utensils. Taking the whole of the federal budget and breaking it into a pie chart for the different expenditures (defense, social services, infrastructure) *divides* the budget. You can classify an entire student body by freshman, sophomore, junior, and senior. You can them divide the classes by gender, major, and along many other lines.

Argumentation and Persuasion

Most texts use these terms interchangeably, but they indicate two similar but nonetheless distinct aspects of conveying opinion-driven meaning with words.

Speaking of that, here's a tip you can take to the bank and earn a dividend. Whenever you have two words that *seem* to describe the same thing (synonyms), they in fact indicate something slightly different, those lovely nuances of meaning that allow writers to fine-tune the picture into crystal clarity. Earlier we looked at the difference between "verb" and "predicate." Words have precise meanings. Use them as correctly as you can. For instance, consider the movement of using your legs to propel yourself from point A to point B. We call it a "walk," but there are many ways to describe this motion: saunter, ambulate, trundle, traipse, stagger, skip, hop, tread, parade, march, stride, hike, trek, amble, mosey, tromp, stomp, tiptoe, lumber, falter, shuffle, waddle, sneak, trot, and more. Each suggests something different. All words work this way.

Back to the main topic.

Both argumentation and persuasion refer a writer's (or speaker's) attempt to present the reader (or audience) a decided point of view on an arguable, and often controversial, topic with the intention of convincing them that their position is correct. You want to get them on your side. If you can't do that, you want to at least open their minds for serious consideration of your viewpoint.

Here's how the two words differ. Argumentation refers to doing this *primarily* through an appeal to *logic and reason*. You present your case from the head/heart to the head, emphasis on head. Persuasion *mainly* appeals to the *emotions*, going from the heart/head to the heart, emphasis on heart. In argumentative prose, you'll often do both in combination, but one will usually take prominence, even if it's 50.1 percent to 49.9 percent. Evidence and logic can cement a case, but tugging the heart strings can also serve as a powerful "convincer."

Generally, for written arguments, rule of thumb says limit the emotions and stick to the facts, using logic and reason to draw convincing conclusions. In speaking, an appeal to the emotions tends to work best. Of course, these are not mutually exclusive and almost never are. The spoken word has the persuasive advantage over the written word because the speaker can use inflection, attire, appearance, lighting, tone, gesture, visuals, sound, and body language to convey additional meaning outside of the words themselves. Writing doesn't have such semantic versatility, but it has the advantage of presenting the reader with an argument through words that remain on the page or screen, allowing more time for deliberative thought and reflection. Try not to think of this in black-and-white terms, however. Argument and persuasion are not the airtight water compartments on the *Titanic* (look what happened to Leo DiCaprio) but complementary strategies for winning debates.

When you receive an argumentative assignment, make sure that you have an arguable topic. The point seems too obvious to make, but it isn't. Here are a few examples:

Arguable: The death penalty is a proven deterrent to violent crime.
Inarguable: Texas leads the nation in public executions each year.
Arguable: The stock market rallied because the Fed lowered interest rates.
Inarguable: The Fed interest rates are the lowest in history.
Arguable: The electoral college should be abandoned.
Inarguable: The electoral college can produce a presidential winner even though the winning candidate loses the popular vote.
Arguable: Smoking causes cancer and should be banned.
Inarguable: Each year, thousands of people die from lung cancer. Many were heavy smokers.
Arguable: Vaccines do not help to prevent transmission of the COVID-19 virus.
Inarguable: Getting vaccinated statistically improves the odds of staying healthy.

In writing the argumentative essay, your goal is to win. That means you should aim to convince the reader either to believe in your case and agree with you or, at minimum, allow the reader to understand your position and agree that it makes sense. With an open mind, you might be able to convert some of the latter to your side.

If you have a choice, select a topic and position that gives you a decent chance of success. Don't argue for a flat earth or life on Venus. Also, pick a controversial problem that has no obvious solution. For such a case, there will be many answers to the problem. The task as a writer is to make *your* view the most convincing. If you want to argue for the existence of UFOs visiting earth from other regions in outer space, you might have a chance. You could make a credible case. If, on the other hand, you want to convince someone that a spaceship shaped like a pink teapot landed in your backyard today, good luck.

How do you win an argument? Think of a courtroom. Both prosecution and defense come armed with the same information (assuming an even-playing field, which isn't always the case). Each side faces the same jury. Who wins? With some juries, the side that presents the evidence in a more reasonable, compelling way. With others, cases will be won on a play to the emotions. Many guilty people have walked and innocents convicted because of emotional appeals. It works the same with your writing. That's why assessing your audience as best you can proves worthwhile, just like opposing lawyers when they run through the list of potential jurors. During the trial, the good lawyer keeps a special eye on jury selection. Try to do the same through an analysis on who your readers might be and anticipating on how they can best be approached.

In argumentation, you need to do more than what kids do when they fight on the playground, the "did too/did not" back-and-forth. I call this approach "the polemics of the sandbox." You can label any immature and poorly formed case with that putdown, as you would this one: "Oh yeah? Your mother wears combat boots" (although, come to think of it, today that's probably a compliment), which leads to our final Swing Thought:

SWING THOUGHT No. 20: YOU WIN AN ARGUMENT BY PROVIDING THE BEST EVIDENCE IN THE MOST COMPELLING WAY

— Develop your arguable points using reason and logic, plus a play on emotions when appropriate.
— Make your stance clear. Don't equivocate.
— Be thorough in research, both your point of view and the opposition's.

Types of Reasoning

Basically, there are two type of reasoning: *inductive* and *deductive*. If your college or university offers a course in logic, by all means, sign up for it. The logic course I took as a freshman proved invaluable. If you're out of school, find a good book on formal logic. Learning logic will enable you to both win influence and take apart opposing views. You can even become formidable. I can't recommend a course in logic highly enough.

Induction—Reaching conclusions proceeding from specific to general. Think of a pyramid, narrow at the top and broad at the base. An inductive argument makes a number of specific observations and from them derives a broad conclusion made to appear inevitable. Induction should be open-ended beginning with as little prejudice or bias as possible. Follow the evidence, not your feelings. Go where the evidence takes you.

Example:

Observation 1: You notice the birds feeding unusually early and with more urgency.
Observation 2: The weather dial shows a falling barometer.
Observation 3: Clouds have moved in from the north.
Observation 4: The wind has picked up.

Conclusion: It likely will be stormy.

Here's another example of an inductive argument:

Observation 1: Size 10 footprints lead to the front door.
Observation 2: Sole treads reveal a man's work boot with a distinctive pattern, worn at the heels and torn in the soles.
Observation 3: The prints are sunk into the damp soil, indicating a person of substantial heft.
Observation 4: The door has been forced.
Observation 5: The stab wound entered the victim's front left shoulder at 55 degrees.

Conclusion: We are looking for a left-handed, burly man who wears size 10, battered, construction boots whose distinctive treads reveal the Timberland brand.

Example:

Observation 1: The movement of planets and stars follows a predictable order that can be precisely described by math.
Observation 2: Such precision could not come about randomly. It had to be designed.
Observation 3: A design must have a designer.

Conclusion: God exists.

Induction is often (and erroneously) called "deduction." For example, in a Sherlock Holmes story, the detective gathers many clues, then reveals to Dr. Watson the identity of the killer.

Watson: "Holmes, how did you arrive at this conclusion?"

Holmes: "Elementary, my dear Watson. Through simple deduction."

Actually, Mr. Holmes, that method describes *induction*.

Deduction—This type of reasoning begins with a generality in the form of a major premise or general assertion that you hold to be true. You might say deduction stands the pyramid of induction on its head by beginning with a conclusion and from it applying reason to specific instances stemming from the premise.

In a deductive argument, everything depends on the truth of the initial assertion. If the major premise is not true, the entire argument collapses. Technically, the argument may be valid, but it will not be true, as in this example:

> *Premise*: People who win big money in the lottery can't handle it. They always end up broke.
> *Specific application*: John won $5 million in the lottery.
> *Conclusion*: John will go broke because of his newfound wealth.

The argument is valid but not necessarily true. John may in fact be financially responsible and be able to manage a large infusion of cash. Contrary to the major premise, not everyone who wins big ends up broke.

Here's another example of deduction. This time, the conclusion is both valid and true. A true argument will always be valid. The reverse, though, doesn't hold.

> *Premise*: Totalitarianism has been without exception bad for ordinary people.
> *Application*: Venezuela's military junta has violently overthrown the democratically elected government and imposed martial law.
> *Conclusion*: Venezuelans will suffer.

This argument is both valid and true.

A deductive argument rests on the validity of the initial premise.

> *Premise*: All dogs are friendly.
> *Application*: Terry has a dog.
> *Conclusion*: Therefore, Terry's dog will be friendly.

In that simple example, again the reasoning is valid but because it stems from a false premise—not all dogs are friendly—the conclusion is not necessarily so. Terry in fact may have an angry dog that will attack at first approach.

> *Premise*: Conservatives ignore human rights.
> *Application*: Candidate A is a conservative.
> *Conclusion*: Therefore, Candidate A will stomp over people's rights.

Is that premise necessarily true? It's arguable, but isn't that the point? Not all conservatives ignore human rights. For many on the political right, the opposite is true.

Or take one of our inductions from above: There is a God. Let's look at it deductively.

> *Major premise*: There is a God.
> *Application*: Nothing happens without God's permission.
> *Conclusion*: Therefore, the tsunami is God's will.

Valid reasoning but faulty logic. The major premise is not necessarily true. There are many who do not believe in God. We can't accept the conclusion because of this.

Evidence

The best way to convince a reader of your argument is to present irrefutable evidence that supports your position. After all, anyone can take any position on any issue, but who wins? The one who can support his assertions with the most compelling evidence in the most convincing fashion.

Overall, when you boil it down, you can employ only two types of evidence: facts and opinions. The difference between the two may look apparent, but not that much evidence presented as fact is factual. In fact, few things qualify as facts (yes, I deliberately chose the transitional repetition for stylistic effect).

Fact—What is a fact? Here's the best definition you'll ever find: A fact is information that stays the same no matter the source. For example, ask anyone or look up from any source "What day was President John F. Kennedy killed?" The answer will always be November 22, 1963. It's inarguable. Same with the answers to "What team won the 1957 World Series?" "On the U.S. East Coast, from what direction does the sun rise?" and "What happens to water when the temperature dips below 32 degrees Fahrenheit?"

When researching and examining material and especially when you present something in your writing as fact, ask yourself: Would it produce the same answer, no matter who you asked or what reference or source you used? If it's genuinely a fact, the answer will not change.

Opinion—An opinion is information that *can* change and often does as the source changes. There's no disagreement on when and where President Kennedy was killed, but if you ask a cross-section of researchers into the assassination who killed JFK, you will receive such answers as the anti-Castro Cubans in Miami, organized crime, Lee Harvey Oswald, the CIA, a government cabal headed by vice-president Lyndon Johnson, or some combination of these. They are offering opinions. Do not make the mistake of careless reasoning. Interpretations of facts are not facts in themselves. Many writers fall into this trap when presenting a case and declaring a point of view. Opinions live or die by the application of the reasoning and evidence supporting them.

When writing argumentatively, you must take a position on an arguable issue, one where a reasonable, alternate view can be presented. You will share all the best evidence you can muster, including as many facts as you can. In the end, however, you will be offering an opinion or interpretation as an analysis of the factual information. You want to make your argument in a reasonable, believable, and convincing manner. That usually involves persuasion, a play on emotions.

Factual claims work best if they can stand up to these questions:

— Why should the reader believe it?
— Would you expect a disinterested person to believe you?
— Is there enough evidence to support your claims?
— Are your assertions true? How do you know?
— Is this the most likely and believable view?
— Is it the most convincing?

Audience. Whenever you make an argumentative presentation, your readers or audience will be in one of four larger categories: Type 1, they have closed minds with the issue fixed in agreement with you (Type 1a) or closed and opposed, often vehemently (Type 1b). Type 2, they have their minds made up but are open to other points of view. Type 3, they haven't yet decided because they don't care about the issue. Type 4, they have no position but want to learn more.

In most writing situations, you won't have the readers in front of you the way a speaker does with an audience. Sometimes, though, you can make reasonable guesses as to target readers. Try to get as much information as you can, even if you come up empty. At least give the question of readers some thought. Of the four reader categories above, the easiest and most friendly will be Type 1a. There you will be "preaching to the choir." The next best will be Type 4 (they are blank slates, ready to be written upon), followed in degree of difficulty by Type 2 (susceptible to changing their minds), Type 3 (maybe you can create interest), and Type 1b (likely to reject, sometimes with hostility). One thing's for sure. If you truly believe in your case, that will show and you'll have a better time "selling" it.

Here are a few tips in writing the argumentative essay.

— Everything we've said thus far about expository prose applies. A beginning, middle, and end, good mechanics, and so on.
— If given a choice, pick a topic you care about. It will show in the authenticity and sincerity of your presentation.
— Do sufficient research to get yourself up to speed. Draw only upon reliable, reputable sources. Make the research thorough and complete.
— State your position clearly, usually in the opening.
— Document any borrowed material. This includes quotations, paraphrase, and summary of others' words and ideas. Not doing so commits plagiarism.
— Research the opposition's likely counterpoints. This is called the *refutation*. In debate, you need to learn your opponent's position as well as you know your own. What are the likely points they will bring up to shoot down your position? Address them head-on before your opponent can lay claim. The preemptive attack works best.
— Revise, revise, revise.

Borrowing from the Work of Others

On most topics, you will need to research the facts, data, and information. You likely won't be an expert. You might know nothing about it. What do you do? Easy. You go to the experts who do know in the form of borrowing from their work. If you're writing about the need for greater access to health care, Formula One racing, or causes of World War II, read and ask what the experts say. Make use of their expertise.

In my writing career, I've written about countless topics that I knew little to nothing about: from architecture to car design, virtual reality to time travel, health care to baseball, set design in films to organized crime, and many more. That's when I would hit the books or pick up the phone. I'd search the literature and interview experts not just to gather material but to stimulate my own thinking.

With the advent and development of the Internet, research has become easier than ever—and more perilous. At the press of a button, your search engine opens up the best of the world's libraries. Unfortunately, that same key click will also deliver you to the worst the online environment has to offer, those scummy gutters of lies, hysteria, porn, and worse. The convenience also makes it easier to copy and paste. That's fine (up to a point, of course) as long as you *properly document* your sources.

Knowing the meaning of domain extensions can help you judge the reputability of various online sites.

— .com: A commercial site. Often reliable but not always. Commercial sometimes indicates a profit bias. Proceed carefully.
— .edu: An educational institution such as a college or university. Usually reliable and then some.
— .gov: A website owned or operated by government. Often a good source, as long as it's not ideological.
— .org: An organization, association, or other similar group. This once had high reliability, but today anyone can buy a .org domain extension, greatly diluting the trust factor.
— .net: A network operation. Use caution.

One of best ways to get help with citation and documentation is to go online to a writing lab hosted by a reputable school. My personal favorite both for ease of use and comprehensiveness is the Purdue OWL (the university's Online Writing Lab). This site provides straightforward guidelines in general source evaluation, proper documentation, and tips on how to conduct academic research.

Document every source thoroughly *as you go along*. Don't wait until your research is done. You'll end up missing citations and have a logistical nightmare on your hands trying to retrace your data-gathering steps. Back in the day, researching with index cards and on hard copy made the collection and assembly of information more tangible and hands-on. Many good writers still do it this way. Relying strictly on online notation can cause problems, as websites often change content and location of materials. The solution: Read the first sentence in this paragraph.

Most writers know that when they lift quotes from other sources, they need to give credit. The same is true about borrowing *ideas* from others. If the thought is not yours, you need to cite the source.

Writers have these options regarding the work of others:

1. Examine but Do Not Use—You survey the field, read to get "up to speed," but choose not to use the material.

2. Examine and Use—Here you have three options.

   2a. Summary: You present the *gist* of the idea giving the main point. You can summarize an entire book in just a few words. Here's a summary of F. Scott Fitzgerald's *The Great Gatsby*: "A *nouveau riche* man desperately attempts to recreate the past, but he finds redemption of his past mistakes impossible, leading to a tragic end." State the summary *in your own words*.

   2b. Paraphrase: Like summary but with more detail. Paraphrasing an idea from the original source, you present the main idea plus other supporting points. Again, a paraphrase must be *in your own words*. Here's a paraphrase of *The Great Gatsby*: "A *nouveau riche* man discovers that in a desperate attempt to repeat the past, he can't redeem the mistakes of the past. When Gatsby learns that Daisy, his former lover, lives across Long Island Sound from his mansion, he tries to woo her despite the fact that she's married. His newfound fortune, made illicitly, gives him an inroad into her heady world of wealth, society, and position. Gatsby learns the harsh lesson about the inviolate nature of the past in the most tragic way." Notice the paraphrase keeps the main point then reinforces it with supplementary observations.

   2c. Direct Quote: Borrowing the actual words from another source. Don't overuse quotations. Save quotes for passages that are so memorable, insightful, or knowledgeable that you couldn't improve on the original. The judicious use of a good quote strengthens material the way a good spice complements a recipe. Just enough salt does the job. Too much ruins the meal. Same with quotes. Also, a research paper that consists of mostly lifted material reveals laziness on the part of the writer. "The Giant Quotation That Filled My Paper" will make an awful horror story for both reader and writer. When lifting quotes, *triple-check for accuracy*. Inserting mistakes or words into a quotation that aren't present in the original is careless and unacceptable.

Most style books will have proper citation formats, which are also available online. The major style sheets are:

MLA (Modern Language Association)—Used in the humanities.

APA (American Psychological Association)—For citations in the social sciences.

Chicago or CMS (Chicago Manual of Style)—Used for citations in published work.

Plagiarism

A word about using the words or thoughts from other sources without giving credit: *Don't. Simply D-O-N-T!*

Don't even think about doing it.

Plagiarizing is literary theft, writing's most serious crime. Careers have been lost and students have been thrown out of school because of this. You don't want to take the chance. You'll get caught, and it's never worth it. The Internet, search engines, and the ease of the cut-and-paste function may tempt you to "borrow" without attribution, but the same technology also helps in picking out stolen words. Keep it above board. If in any doubt, consult a research librarian, your instructor, or your editor. If you're still not sure, cite the source. That way, you can never go wrong.

In Review

Swing Thought from Chapter Ten

20. You win an argument by presenting the best evidence in the most logical and compelling fashion.

Writing Prompts

1. Come up with five arguable topics that would make for suitable research papers. Why do these topics interest you? Why did you select them? What would your point of view be on each? What evidence would you use?
2. What is your experience using outside sources and citations? Do you feel comfortable finding useful material? Are you familiar with the conditions required for proper citation?

3. What are your thoughts about plagiarism? Do you recognize it as a serious problem? Have you ever done it? Be honest.

Reading Suggestions

1. *Stolen Words: Forays Into the Origins and Ravages of Plagiarism* by Thomas Mallon—This book puts plagiarism in its proper place as writing's Cardinal Sin.
2. "Six Scandalous Plagiarism Stories That You Should Know," www.plagiarism.org—A sobering look at how six people—a senior director of the National Security Council, a comedian, a martial arts competitor, a reporter, an architect, and a college professor—ruined their careers via literary theft.
3. "Exploring Why Students Plagiarize" by Allison Berryhill, www.edutopia.org—Especially pertinent to all those engaged in academic research.

CHAPTER ELEVEN

The Last Word

I hope the advice shared in *Write It Real* has the done job of taking you from where you started as a writer, at level X, and brings you to at least X+1. Anything above that you can consider gravy.

Real writing speaks directly to its readers, presenting words to them, at them, for them. It begins with a writer realizing that the art and science of crafting words and fashioning them at optimal best can be traced to a definable, manageable process that can be taught, learned, practiced, and mastered to produce accomplished prose, on demand. *Real* writing doesn't depend on inspiration, though the muse will always be welcome, but on the writer's *decision* to write, usually based on the need caused by a deadline or a request.

The heart of this book and the core of your creative work as a writer center around the writing *process*, those five steps that tame the wilderness of prose into manageability. Too often, people, even would-be writers, think of writing as a mysterious skill handed down by druids and high priests and priestesses of secret societies; conveyed in rituals, handshakes, and coded passwords; and available only to initiates who have gone through a long and arduous hazing before they can be considered "made."

Not so.

You know now, in the unlikely event you didn't before, that writing is nothing like that. Writing assumes the mantle of most every other human skill. It's teachable and "learnable" and can be conveyed from one to another as a combination of intelligent instruction and, mainly, diligent application.

That's the only way you can master any skill, be it playing a guitar, learning a new language, becoming a skier, or writing. Instruction points the way, but it can't actually do the walking or heavy lifting. That's up to you. The basic requirements of the practitioner: openness, diligence, determination, and practice. Hours, days, months, and a lifetime of practice. From whence do you think the word "practitioner" derives?

I recall an interview with the classical composer Igor Stravinsky (1882–1971), in my view the most important figure in 20th-century classical music without peer as a composer, conductor, and pianist. Late in life, he sat down with a student protégé as a film crew documented master and pupil sharing music and notes. At one point, Stravinsky says to his acolyte that he, referring to himself, still has so much to learn. Later, in an interview, he reveals that he still tries to practice at least four hours a day. Before a concert, he works on the program four to six hours a day!

Think about that. From the outside, you'd think that such a giant, having conquered the known musical world, would have achieved all, and yet from the inside, you hear Stravinsky in his late 80s speak of new worlds to explore—learning, always learning, refining his technique, improving, refreshing muscle memory, staying sharp, flexible, and loose. The same holds true for other masters of skill, be it monks, runners, actors, or machinists. And writers.

I've had millions of words published and performed in all sorts of media in a professional career that goes back to 1975. Here I am, these many years later, still a voracious reader, still writing with the goal of at least a thousand words daily, still ever on the hunt to acquire new and exciting information, to express and share new insights.

In that light, ask yourself where your passion lies. How much do you want it?

In the larger sense, our task in life is to find the work "[your] soul must have," as Alice Walker says of her mother in her brilliant essay "In Search of Our Mother's Gardens," along with Orwell's "Shooting an Elephant" and the columns of H.L. Mencken among my favorite pieces of 20th-century expository prose.

In saying this, let me be quick to declare that you do not need to have a devotion for writing. You may not even like it. In fact, it might be a chore ranking up there with waxing the car, clipping the cat's nails, and doing a backload of laundry. No problem. It makes you like the majority of people who hate to write but, for whatever reason, must. The demands of the classroom and the workplace come quickly to mind.

It's okay not to enjoy writing. It's fine even hating to write because of the process as I've explained it in this book. However, anyone with a modicum of smarts can apply these steps to writing and begin to sparkle on the page, irrespective of feeling.

The Writing Process

In review, the writing process consists of five steps: Noise, Prewriting, First Draft, Rest, and Revision.

Noise—The writer "quiets" as many of the distractions and impediments that form obstacles (noise) to their work, taking the time to figure out the conditions under which they do their best work, then trying to replicate those conditions as best they can, given the constraints of time, schedules, individual circumstances, and a myriad other responsibilities.

The quest for optimal conditions and atmosphere won't always be perfect. Maybe it never is. Doesn't matter. The point is, if you need calm, try to find it. If you need crowds and company, go to a place that delivers them. It's surprising how few writers other than serious pros worry about noise. Truly, it's the first thing a writer needs to address.

Poet Robert Creeley once said, "The necessary environment is that which secures the artist in the way that lets [them] be in the world in a most fruitful manner." Creeley himself required a "very kind of secure quiet," as he put it. "I usually have some music playing, a kind of drone that I like, as relaxation" (from *Writers & Poets*, March/April issue, "The Literary Life," by Alexandra Enders).

Toni Morrison prefers the sterility of a motel room. Ben Franklin wrote in his bathtub. D.H. Lawrence did his best work outside, under a tree. Marcel Proust wrote in bed.

Any writer who is serious about it will search for the "necessary environment."

If you're not doing it, well, begin doing it. As I put it in Chapter One, you have to get "ready to write."

Prewriting—This planning stage refers to everything, literally everything, that goes on with a writer, mentally and physically, before beginning a first draft. Writers who claim they don't outline or plan don't know what they're saying because they don't understand the process. Their writing will provide the evidence of that. Even if you began to write a minute after getting an assignment, in that one minute, your brain begins to work on the problem. That's how it is with any creative task. Conceptually, the planning immediately begins.

Gathering material and putting it in some kind of order form the bulk of prewriting. If you're writing from personal experience, you have most of the material stored in your memory. The task then becomes one of ferreting out the relevant details, some of which will come immediately to mind. Best to take notes when that happens. You might also try one or more of the strategies referred to in this book.

Brainstorming involves jotting down ideas associated with the topic as rapidly as they come to mind. You don't evaluate. That will come later. Putting these down in note form, whether in longhand or on a computer, serves two important purposes. First, it provides a record of your thinking. Second, you'll find that memories unlock other memories that would have remained buried had you not taken the time to take notes.

In *free writing*, you begin scribbling phrases and sentences that pertain to the subject, however remotely. You'll find that certain words lead to other associations that may surprise or be off topic. No matter. Free writing doesn't evaluate. It spits out words as if from a machine gun, consecutive if disjointed prose that helps to unlock material. Again, making notes preserves the ideas, giving them a concrete form.

When *brainstorming* and *free writing* conclude, review what you wrote. There will be a lot of chaff that you can immediately toss. Doubtless, though, you'll find some precious nuggets that will be of use for your outline and when diving into the first draft.

Ask yourself how much you know about the topic. Often, you'll need to do research. It's best to have a specific aim in mind when you investigate a topic. If you're writing about voting rights, for example, have a narrow focus, perhaps confining it to a particular election cycle. The general topic will be too big to handle in its entirety. A writer can almost never narrow down enough. This is especially true for the developing writer. You can't say everything, but you can say enough about something.

Once your material is gathered, fathom out the proper order. Outlining is nothing more than bringing the various pieces of material into focus and establishing an overall point or theme, what I call a controlling idea (CI). The outline is a preliminary or provisional grasp of the material. Nothing more. It needn't be some elaborate, formal structure. As you recall, I mentioned how a strict or formal outline can often hem in the writer, as in a straightjacket. A few main ideas and notes on the supporting development are usually enough. The CI determines the overall direction of the writing, and unless you can state your CI in a succinct sentence, you're not ready to write.

First Draft—I don't call this "writing." A first draft is just that: First. Draft. There will be a second, third, fourth, and as many as needed until you've fashioned the material in its best order and your deadline is at hand. That's why I say there is no such thing as "writing." There's only rewriting. Virtually every published piece you've ever read, if not literally every one, is the product of revision and rewrite.

The goal of a first draft is to get your thoughts down on paper or screen, from start to finish, as best you can. Try to complete it with as few stops as possible. Having a reasonably finished draft now gives you something on which you can work. Don't get bogged down by trying for the perfect word, sentence, or paragraph. Write it the best you can and save the evaluations and improvements for when you revise.

Rest—Time to get away. After writing a first draft, you need to cap the pen or walk away from the keyboard and as best as you can forget about the work. Many writing texts never mention this need, probably because they think it's self-evident. It's not. Too many times I've seen writers take a first draft and immediately try to fix it. Often, a writer will attempt to draft and revise at the same time, resulting in a brainstorm and not the kind you want.

Taking time off from the work, as much as your deadline will allow, enables you to return to it with fresh eyes, taking up the task of revision as if you're looking at someone's else work. As you gain experience as a writer, this will get easier. You'll develop more of a tough skin and not be so quick to "fall in love" with your words just because you wrote them.

Revision—Literally, it means to re-see, and revision is by far the most difficult part of writing to learn to do well. You'll spend a lifetime getting better at it. You learn by seeing it done in the form of intelligent feedback and mostly by doing it. Do it enough, and you will begin to get the "feel" for good writing.

In revising, you want to take a dispassionate view of the writing. Do the words say what you wanted to say? Is there a better way to convey the point? Did you leave anything out? Are sentences or sections out of place? Is there extraneous material, that is deadwood (DW)? The answer to that last one is yes. Always yes. No matter how good that draft copy is, guaranteed DW lurks in the prose. Again, remember Orwell's Third Rule of Writing from "Politics and the English Language": "If it is possible to cut a word out, always cut it out."

"Always," he says. "Always" allows for no exceptions. Be ruthless with DW.

Never revise unless the change you make improves the copy. Never make a change simply for change's sake. Check for proper grammar and spelling. Find the typos. Like DW, a few will stubbornly remain hidden, as if they put on camouflage. Be on the hunt. If you don't find them, a reviewer, editor, or instructor will.

Before you finish, proofread carefully. Adopt this motto: "You can always proof one last time." Guarantee: Even with the *nth* proof, you'll still be finding dumb little mistakes.

Hand in your work in the format required by the assignor. Pay attention to neatness and legibility. Make that first impression a good one. When choosing which English idiom to adopt, something you'll do at the outset, keep in mind the expectations of the receiver of your work—readers, assignors, editors.

Most professional, commercial, and academic outlets will want Standard American English (SAE). Some will allow non-SAE dialects, writing groups for example. Whether its SAE, African American Vernacular English (AAVE), or some other English dialect, it will be your choice as a writer. These forms are equally valid and only find preference within the cultural, editorial, and conceptual contexts. Knowing the preferences of your recipient will help you in making that choice.

Swing Thoughts

I encapsulated some of this book's most important points in what I called Swing Thoughts. These are succinct guidelines that provide direction without getting anyone lost in thought.

1. You must be ready to write.
2. Writing is hard work. You must commit to the heavy lifting.
3. The best way to learn a skill is to practice it. That holds true with writing.
4. Mature writers don't wait for inspiration. They *decide* to write.
5. Make sure you fully understand assignments.
6. Serious writers never miss a deadline.
7. An outline is a *preliminary* grasp of your material, your best guess.
8. Write for the reader. Do anything that will help the reader.
9. You can't write a "bad" first draft. Impossible. Revision makes this is so.
10. Don't make a change for change's sake. Have a good reason for every edit.
11. Paragraphs state main ideas generally and develop them specifically.
12. Check the relevance of your developmental material, especially examples.
13. An effective paragraph is unified, coherent, and complete.
14. Your introduction gives the reader a *hint* at what's to come.
15. The body of the essay is where *development* of the CI takes place.
16. The conclusion should provide the *sense of an ending*.
17. Transitions (TR) supply connections between ideas, giving unity and flow.
18. The most important grammatical skill is recognizing subjects and verbs.
19. Keep a list of all errors pointed out in feedback.
20. You win arguments with best evidence presented with logic and reason.

Writing Magic

Do you remember the yellow "magic pill" from Chapter Six? When you take that little pill, you instantly become a proficient writer.

Yeah. It doesn't exist, but I gave you the next best thing: the humble paragraph. Without question, the paragraph is the basic building block of nonfiction expository prose because it's the first "level" of writing (moving up from the individual letter, to the word, phrase, clause, etc.) where you find true development.

That's how prose runs. You state a general idea, then develop it specifically. Having the ideas, good ones, rarely is the problem. We all live in our heads, and the thoughts we use to make sense of the world are predominately interesting, on occasion even profound. Ah, but try getting those thoughts out of your head, onto the page, keeping as much of the nuance, depth, and profundity as possible. There's the rub, as the Bard would say.

That's where the paragraph comes into vital use. A paragraph is a *group* of *related* sentences that *together* express a *single, unified* idea. Look at the words in italics. A paragraph isn't just any "group of sentences." It's a group of them flying in formation on a bombing run to the same objective. The topic sentence (TS) of the paragraph states the general idea, with the subsequent sentences providing the supporting details and illustrations.

I'll flat out say it: If you can write solid, effective paragraphs, guess what? You are a WRITER!

A well-honed paragraph possesses three qualities:

(1) It's *unified*, with all the information supporting the TS. (2) It's *coherent*, with no irrelevant material. No matter how interesting extraneous material may be, if it's in the wrong place, boot it. (3) It's *complete*; that is, the TS is fully developed. Write paragraphs that have these three qualities, and you're on your way to writing success.

Such effective paragraphs build one upon the other, solid blocks held together within and attached to each other without through another one of those "magic" devices: transitions (TR).

TR fill the gaps in writing the way a bridge connects two pieces of land divided by a gorge. Words such as "thus, nonetheless, in contrast, however," and so many more provide lubrication, keeping ideas flowing smoothly and not jamming up. Guaranteed that there are TR in your work. Look for them. Circle them. Do you have enough of them? Often, when the writing seems choppy and bumpy, it's because it lacks proper transitioning.

The Rhetorical Modes

As a prose writer, you'll make frequent use of the various writing patterns or strategies I call the rhetorical modes of exposition. The three most important, found in nearly every piece of prose ever written, are description, example, and narration. When you combine the three, you have the essential ingredients for good, great, and even brilliant writing.

Description—The 5Ws and H born of the newsroom: who, what, when, where, why, and sometimes how. Have the answers to these, and you've run the descriptive checklist. *Objective* description (denotation) presents a straightforward view of how an object, place, or situation looks. *Subjective* description (connotation) gives the reader an "emotional feel" for the thing or event.

Example—The pulsing heart of prose. Exemplification offers specific illustrations and details to support general statements. General-to-specific, that is the essence and the movement of nonfiction prose. Nothing's more frustrating to the reader than vague, overgeneralized writing. Exemplification functions in writing as the focus ring does on a camera or projector.

Narrative—Telling a story, something you know about and have loved since you were a kid. Where description is spatial, narrative is chronological, events taking place in time. Your default strategy for narrative is to stick to a past-to-present-to-future chronology, a "this happened, then that happened, followed by the next thing" approach. Keep tense consistent.

Comparison and Contrast—The first notes similarities between objects and items. The second lists differences. This is a "one-in-terms-of-the-other" technique, something you do every time you compare heads of lettuce in the produce section of a supermarket. It works well for writing, too.

Cause and Effect—Cause answers the question "why?" Why did the space shuttle blow up? Why did the stock market crash? Why did the Patriots win the Super Bowl? Effect addresses "what if?" What if we cash in our IRAs? What if we let Peter get his driver's license? What if Germany had won World War II?

Process Analysis—Explains how to do something. It shares the ingredients and factors involved, the steps to take, the sequence to follow, and the actions needed. When you write an essay titled "How to Change a Diaper," you're dealing in process.

Definition—Two kinds. There's the *denotive*, dictionary definition, and there's the *connotative* or "emotional" definition. You can define bourbon as a "distilled spirit." You can also call it "the burnt-amber liquid that reveals the truth of existence."

Classification and Division—Another technique that notes differences and similarities, useful in analyzing large, complex subjects. Classification starts with disparate items and places them into ranks. Division begins with a singularity and breaks it up into component parts. You *classify* students by grades or, in college, rank. You *divide* a pie into slices.

Argumentation—Also called persuasion, found in much of writing, fiction, non-fiction, and poetry. Argumentation takes a decided point of view (POV) on a controversial topic, usually one with many possible positions. You defend your position using logic, evidence, and emotional appeal while attacking alternate arguments. In writing argumentatively, you want to win the reader over to your POV.

The "Stumble" Words

Most every handbook, stylebook, and stylesheet I've ever examined includes a glossary of usage, explaining the words that give writers trouble.

I've not included a full-length usage glossary in this book because I haven't written a handbook. There are enough of those, and plenty of good ones. That said, however, in my long career as a writer, editor, and teacher—involving countless thousands of writings and thousands of college students—I do have my Top Ten "pet peeve" list.

These are the "stumble" words that I have seen most regularly botched. I say this both anecdotally and "scientifically." As for the latter ("latter" and "former" were candidates for the Stumble List), for many years I kept a record of the words that gave writers the most trouble, taken from examples in actual use. Conscience bids me to include them here for you, listed in alphabetical order.

Here, for your pleasure and scholarly cultivation, I present Valenti's Top 10 Stumble List:

> *accept* and *except*: Accept means to receive. "The team accepted Kayla." Except signifies exclusion. "Everyone made the cut except Tommy."
>
> *affect* and *effect*: The first is a verb, meaning to influence. "How did turnout affect the vote?" The second indicates a result or accomplishment. "The Colonists effected a revolution."
>
> *among* and *between*—Use among when dealing with three or more persons or things. Use between if there are only two: "Among the Three Musketeers …" "Between the two of us …" Some usage manuals will allow between to refer more than two. This is a relatively recent development and not commonly accepted. Generally, the surest usage will be as I originally stated.

complement and *compliment*—The first, with an "e," means something goes well with or gets along (compatible) with something else. Spelling the word with an "i," sends praise or compatibility. "Peanut butter complements jelly perfectly." "Prof. Ullman complimented Dan on his work."

firstly, secondly, thirdly, and so forth—Drop the "ly," which is British usage.

irregardless and *regardless*—Regularly botched. "Irregardless" makes no sense. It's a double negative. A word can't self-negate, that is, commit linguistic suicide. *Regardless* is the proper usage.

its and *it's*—The granddaddy of all incorrect, stumbling usage, causing more guessing than fantasy football. "Its" without the apostrophe is possessive, as in "The cat loved its new toy." Use with the apostrophe, it's, and you have a contraction for "it is." And while we're at it, there is no such word as "its'." If you learn no other set of homonyms and proper usage, learn this one.

literally—Means exactly as stated. Use the word when you don't want the reader to mistake something as figurative. "He literally ate the entire bunch of grapes." Misuse occurs as an intensifier, such as "Catcher, pitcher, and centerfield form the literal backbone of defensive baseball." No. There's no actual bone material connecting the three positions on a baseball diamond.

principal and principle—The first refers to the CEO, manager, or head official of an organization or enterprise. It also means "a sum of money." Principle means a precept, law, or belief. "Coltrara served as school principal for three years." "Renzi stuck to her principles."

respectfully and *respectively*—The first means showing respect. The second means "in that order." "In China, children treat their elders respectfully." "Williams and Mantle, respectively, played left and center for the American League All Stars."

Research and Citations

You're familiar with Internet search engines, and they often provide enough material for many research projects—many, maybe most, but not all. It's good practice to learn how to use libraries to do research, and one of the most important persons is the research librarian. I used to advise my students that after meeting your new roommate, the next most important person on campus to meet and greet is the research librarian. Make the research expert one of your best friends.

Libraries contains vast archives, particularly material that might not be available online such as out-of-print books, periodicals, pamphlets, company newspapers, unabridged reference books, and other obscure works. Examine bibliographies to learn of a given's field's most expert sources.

The most simple principle in citation: Cite anytime you borrow someone else's ideas or words. If you're not sure, ask. When in doubt, always cite the source.

If you don't properly document borrowed material, you commit writing's worst offense, plagiarism. Stealing the thoughts or words of others, a crime that occurs when you don't give credit, will never be okay. DON'T EVEN THINK OF PLAGIARIZING! Document all use of outside sources.

One Last Word

In ending, let me share one final piece of advice.

Whether you enjoy writing or think of it as a horrible task, mastery over this skill is within the reach of anyone of reasonable ability willing to make the effort. Good writing never emerges from a casual, "good enough" attitude. It's the product of a determination to improve, diligent practice, and continually learning through mistakes.

As social beings, humans have a built-in affinity for language and words owing to our need to communicate and connect with each other. Communication, along with taming fire, has been handed down through the millennia of civilization and prior as a life-or-death survival technique. We quickly learned as a species that to communicate well meant forward progress through the sharing of discovery plus cultural enrichment through writing's ability to preserve the past.

This affinity and ability lie within each of us. Unfortunately, the remarkable potential of that inborn need to communicate, to write, often finds itself bludgeoned by a variety of forces, including poor teaching, a de-emphasis of writing's importance, a relentless societal pressure ever toward the visual, and technology's distraction via ease of use and sensory overload.

The potential to improve as a writer exists now, in this moment, within you. You can activate that potential through the processes and strategies shared in this book. There's no ceiling that limits how much you can improve and how much you can accomplish.

All that's left is to get on and get at it.

I'll be with you all the way.

Index

www.ingramcontent.com/pod-product-compliance
Lightning Source LLC
Chambersburg PA
CBHW071414290326
41932CB00047B/2955